GOD'S DESIGN FOR MARRIAGE

A BLUEPRINT FOR LASTING LOVE IN CHRIST

DR. DEBORAH SKOMBA

God's Design for Marriage: A Blueprint for Lasting Love in Christ

Copyright © 2024 by Dr. Deborah Skomba

All rights reserved. No part of this book may be reproduced or transmitted in any form or by any means, electronic or mechanical, including photocopying, recording, any information storage, and retrieval system, without written permission of the author except in the case of brief quotations embodied in critical articles and reviews.

For information on distribution rights, royalties, derivative works, or licensing opportunities on behalf of this content or work, please get in touch with the publisher at the address below:

Farmhouse Publishings, LLC,
P.O. Box 333
Spearfish, SD 57783

Scripture quotations are from the ESV®Bible (The Holy Bible, English Standard Version®), copyright© 2001 by Crossway Bibles, a publishing ministry of Good News Publishers. Used by permission. All rights reserved. Scripture quotations from The Authorized (King James) Version. Rights in the Authorized Version in the United Kingdom are vested in the Crown. Reproduced by permission of the Crown's patentee, Cambridge University Press. Scripture texts in this work are taken from the New American Bible, revised edition© 2010, 1991, 1986, 1970 Confraternity of Christian Doctrine, Washington, D.C., and are used by permission of the copyright owner. All Rights Reserved. No part of the New American Bible may be reproduced in any form without permission in writing from the copyright owner. Scripture quotations marked (NIV) are taken from the Holy Bible, New International Version®, NIV®. Copyright © 1973, 1978, 1984, 2011 by Biblica, Inc.™ Used by permission of Zondervan. All rights reserved worldwide. www.zondervan.com. The "NIV" and "New International Version" are trademarks registered in the United States Patent and Trademark Office by Biblica, Inc.™ Scripture quotations marked (TLB) are taken from The Living Bible, copyright © 1971 by Tyndale House Foundation. Used by permission of Tyndale House Publishers, Carol Stream, Illinois 60188. All rights reserved.

Although the author and publisher have tried to ensure that the information and advice in this book were correct and accurate at press time, the author and publisher do not assume and disclaim any liability to any party for any loss, damage, or disruption caused by acting upon the information in this book or by errors or omissions, whether such errors or omissions result from negligence, accident, or any other cause.

ISBN: 979-8-9918470-1-8

Interior Layout by Heidi Caperton

Printed in the United States of America

To my beloved husband, Michael, whose unwavering love and support inspire me every day. Your commitment to our marriage has shown me the beauty of Christ–centered love; together, we continue to build a legacy of faith.

To all couples seeking to deepen their connection and embrace God's Design For Marriage—may you find strength, guidance, and joy in these pages as you navigate your journey together.

TABLE OF CONTENTS

INTRODUCTION XI

CHAPTER ONE: FORGIVENESS AND GRACE 1
   UNDERSTANDING THE POWER OF FORGIVENESS IN MARRIAGE 7
   EXTENDING GRACE AND MERCY TO ONE ANOTHER 10
   HEALING PAST HURTS AND REBUILDING TRUST 11

**CHAPTER TWO: FOUNDATIONS OF FAITH –
GOD'S BLUEPRINT FOR MARRIAGE** 19
   GOD'S ORIGIN OF MARRIAGE 22
   GOD'S PURPOSE OF MARRIAGE 23
   SIGNIFICANCE IN GOD'S DESIGN FOR MARRIAGE 24

CHAPTER THREE: UNDERSTANDING GOD'S PLAN FOR MARRIAGE . . 33
   EXPLORING BIBLICAL FOUNDATIONS OF MARRIAGE 35
   THE ROLES OF HUSBAND AND WIFE ACCORDING TO SCRIPTURE 39
   THE IMPORTANCE OF COMMITMENT AND COVENANT 44

CHAPTER FOUR: COMMUNICATION IN MARRIAGE 51
   EFFECTIVE COMMUNICATION SKILLS BASED ON
   BIBLICAL PRINCIPLES 53
   STRATEGIES FOR ACTIVE LISTENING AND EXPRESSING
   FEELINGS RESPECTFULLY 55
   RESOLVING CONFLICTS IN A HEALTHY AND CHRIST-
   CENTERED MANNER 57

CHAPTER FIVE: NURTURING INTIMACY **69**
    PHYSICAL, EMOTIONAL, AND SPIRITUAL INTIMACY IN MARRIAGE. . . . 72
    CULTIVATING INTIMACY THROUGH QUALITY TIME
    AND SHARED EXPERIENCES 74
    OVERCOMING OBSTACLES TO INTIMACY 75

CHAPTER SIX: BUILDING A STRONG FOUNDATION **87**
    ESTABLISHING COMMON GOALS AND VALUES AS A COUPLE 90
    STRENGTHENING MARRIAGE THROUGH PRAYER AND FAITH 94
    INVESTING IN THE RELATIONSHIP FOR THE LONG TERM 97

CHAPTER SEVEN: OVERCOMING CHALLENGES TOGETHER **107**
    ADDRESSING COMMON CHALLENGES FACED BY COUPLES 110
    DEALING WITH EXTERNAL PRESSURES AND INFLUENCES. 111
    SEEKING GUIDANCE AND SUPPORT FROM GOD AND THE
    CHRISTIAN COMMUNITY 112

CHAPTER EIGHT: EMBRACING GOD'S DESIGN FOR MARRIAGE **121**
    CELEBRATING THE BEAUTY AND PURPOSE OF MARRIAGE 124
    LIVING OUT GOD'S PLAN FOR MARRIAGE IN DAILY LIFE. 126
    LEAVING A LASTING LEGACY OF LOVE 129

YOUR JOURNEY CONTINUES **139**
    EMBRACING YOUR DREAM MARRIAGE 142

RESOURCES **145**

ENDNOTES **169**

ABOUT THE AUTHOR **171**

"Submit to one another out of reverence for Christ. Wives, submit yourselves to your own husbands as you do to the Lord. For the husband is the head of the wife as Christ is the head of the church, his body, of which he is the Savior. Now as the church submits to Christ, so also wives should submit to their husbands in everything.

Husbands love your wives, just as Christ loved the church and gave himself up for her to make her holy, cleansing her by the washing with water through the word, and to present her to himself as a radiant church, without stain or wrinkle or any other blemish, but holy and blameless. In this same way, husbands ought to love their wives as their own bodies. He who loves his wife loves himself. After all, no one ever hated their own body, but they feed and care for their body, just as Christ does the church—for we are members of his body. 'For this reason, a man will leave his father and mother and be united to his wife, and the two will become one flesh.' This is a profound mystery—but I am talking about Christ and the church. However, each one of you also must love his wife as he loves himself, and the wife must respect her husband."

~ Ephesians 5:21-33 (ESV)

Welcome!

In a world where trends and values are always changing, the institution of marriage needs to remain a shining example of the power of love and commitment. Here, we'll explore the heart of intimacy, uncover the secrets to lasting love, and strengthen your faith in the sacred covenant of marriage.

I've prayed for you to find me, but even more than that, I've prayed for you to discover what God has in mind for your marriage. I'm convinced that the dream marriage you've always wanted can come to life only when Christ is at the heart of your relationship with your spouse.

As a Christian counselor specializing in Christ–centered marriages, I have noticed that children flourish under the guidance of devoted, faith-driven parents. While this book isn't about parenting tips or strategies to change your spouse, it aims to help strengthen the foundation of your marriage, which in turn positively impacts your family life.

This is your essential guidebook, your blueprint for marriage, where each experience reveals the insights and wisdom you need to nurture a stronger, Christ-centered relationship. As your guide, I will help you navigate important milestones, enabling you to tackle challenges and enhance your blueprint for marriage and spiritual connection, creating a meaningful way of life.

You will study the core principles that underpin a marriage centered on Christ. Acknowledging the value of clear communication, the transformational potential of forgiveness, the beauty of intimacy, and the strength found in prayer are all necessary steps. You will be inspired to embrace God's viewpoint on marriage, actively seeking His guidance during both challenging and fruitful times while nurturing a relationship that glorifies Him in every aspect.

This book isn't just a blueprint — it's an invitation to take action. It encourages you to dive deep into your marriage, reignite the spark of love and commitment, and welcome the countless blessings that come from entrusting your relationships to God's caring hands.

Whether you're just starting your journey as newlyweds or are long-time partners looking to strengthen your marriage, I invite you to join me on this transformative journey.

By doing so, you'll fortify your marriage and draw you closer to the One who destined your union from the start.

Be still beloved; this is where faith, love, and commitment meet.

This book centers on your marriage and its impact on your family dynamics. From my experience in Christian counseling, I've seen that when parents prioritize their relationship, it brings healing to the whole family. When parents foster their bond and build essential skills for self-love and caring for each other, their children reap the rewards. This establishes a foundation of love that radiates outward, creating a loving environment that benefits everyone.

It goes beyond mere theories; it's about applying practical strategies that encourage effective communication, resolve conflicts, and enhance intimacy.

It is a call to action to prioritize your relationship with Christ, recognize Him as your marriage's foundation, and deepen your understanding of God's divine plan for marriage.

When you long to renew your commitment, you'll begin by reassessing your marriage vows. Only then will you start to appreciate the sacredness of the covenant you have entered into. For those who are navigating challenges or healing from wounds in your relationship, I pray this book will bring much-needed healing, reconciliation, and restoration.

Aim high! Look up!

Get ready to deepen your faith in God and put your trust in His plan for your marriage, finding strength and hope in His promises, feeling empowered and equipped to navigate the ups and downs of married life with grace, wisdom, and resilience. May the Holy Bible and this book serve as beacons of hope and inspiration, uplifting you toward a marriage deeply rooted in faith, love, and grace.

With love and blessings,

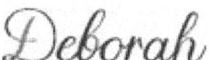

INTRODUCTION

OVERVIEW OF THE BOOK'S PURPOSE AND APPROACH

Why do we need a book on God's design for marriage?

This book is written with God's design for marriage in mind and offers a timeless blueprint rooted in Biblical principles. It provides you with guidance on building a Christ–centered relationship that withstands the test of time and strengthens family unity. You'll discover how embracing God's design can transform your relationship into a source of strength, love, and lasting fulfillment.

While there are so many books out there to help marriages, marriages are still struggling—even among those who seek to honor God in their relationships. When issues go unaddressed, they can reach a point of no return. This book is relevant because it sheds light on God's healing power for marriages before and after "I do."

I've experienced it firsthand, and I believe in its life-changing potential. As you read, know that it's not by chance but by God's intervention through His divine grace.

I'd love to share my love story with you.

Years ago, as my then-boyfriend (now husband) and I were contemplating the prospect of engagement, we received wise counsel from a godly friend. He shared with us a timeless truth that would forever shape the course of our relationship: if we were to build a healthy and strong marriage, Christ must be the foundation upon which it is built.

This revelation resonated deeply with us, stirring a desire to align our relationship with God's perfect plan. With Christ at the center, we discovered a source of strength, guidance, and unwavering love that sustained us through the ups and downs, the ebbs and flows, and all the seasons of life.

Through the trials and triumphs of our journey together, you will experience firsthand the life-changing power of a Christ–centered relationship. This life-changing power inspired me to dedicate my life to helping others cultivate marriages that reflect the love, grace, and purpose of a Heavenly Father.

As we recently celebrated 40 years of marriage, we paused for a moment to reflect on the continuing journey that has brought us here so far—a journey marked by joy, laughter, tears, and triumphs. Through it all, it was our commitment to a Christ–centered love that has remained unwavering, allowing us to grow closer together with each passing year.

As a Christian counselor and coach passionate about healthy, strong marriages, I am deeply honored to walk alongside you on this journey. This book provides a blueprint for how to have a lasting love through Christ that is not only enduring but also flourishing marriages that reflect the love, grace, and purpose of a Heavenly Father.

If you are not a believer yet in Jesus Christ as your Savior but feel in your heart that this is what you want to do for your marriage, take the step of faith and say the "*Salvation Prayer*," which can be found in the Resources section at the back of this book. This is your time to begin your journey of healing and transformation with the only Source for healing hearts. You will be equipped with practical tools to honor God in your marriage and life. My prayer will always be for you to walk closer to God each day and every day and with each and every step.

Before you begin your journey through *God's Design for Marriage*, you have a choice: you can hold fast to the truth revealed in Genesis 3:10-19—that even in brokenness, God's love remains steadfast—or you can turn away from God and His truth for your life, marriage, and relationships. Your Choice.

Pick your hard. Marriage is hard, but so is divorce.

Get ready to discover the beauty of unity, the power of mutual love and respect, and the fruitfulness of a marriage rooted in Christ. You will uncover profound truths that transcend fleeting cultural norms, anchoring your relationship in timeless principles. This is your invitation to embrace a unity that strengthens, a love that honors, and a life together that bears lasting fruit. These foundational teachings will enrich your marriage and align it with God's purpose, ensuring it flourishes in every season.

That is why the necessity for a book of this nature arises.

Who is this for?

God's Design for Marriage is for those committed to building healthy, strong, Christ-centered marriages. At the same time, the book's wisdom and insights are beneficial for you but also for others who can particularly benefit from its guidance and encouragement.

This is for engaged couples who are preparing to embark on the journey of marriage. *God's Design for Marriage* offers invaluable insights into the foundational principles of a Christ-centered relationship. By laying a solid foundation rooted in faith, communication, and mutual respect while engaged, you can set yourself up for a lifetime of love and commitment.

This is for newlyweds who are in the early years of marriage and are still filled with excitement but also with unique challenges and adjustments. *God's Design for Marriage* provides newlyweds with practical tools and strategies for transitioning from "I do" to a lifetime of partnership, intimacy, and growth.

This is for couples facing challenges that every marriage encounters along the way, whether it be communication breakdowns, conflicts, or external pressures. *God's Design for Marriage* offers hope and encouragement to you facing challenges, guiding you towards healing, reconciliation, and renewed commitment to your relationship.

This is for seasoned couples. Even if you have been married for many years, you can benefit from the timeless wisdom found within these pages. *God's Design for Marriage* offers opportunities for reflection, growth, and renewal, helping seasoned couples deepen their connection, reignite their passion, and rediscover the joy of a Christ-centered marriage.

This is for those considering marriage in the future. *God's Design for Marriage* serves as a valuable resource for understanding the biblical principles and values that support a healthy, strong, and lasting marriage. By gaining insight into what it means to build a marriage centered on Christ, you can make informed decisions about your future relationships.

This is for those couples seeking spiritual growth beyond practical advice and guidance. *God's Design for Marriage* offers you an opportunity for spiritual growth and enrichment. Through biblical teachings, reflection questions, and personal anecdotes, you can deepen your faith, strengthen your relationship with God, and experience the transformative power of His love in your marriage.

At its core, this book is for anyone wanting to build a marriage that truly reflects our Heavenly Father's love, grace, and purpose. Whether you're newly engaged, navigating the challenges of married life, or seeking to enrich your relationship with God and each other, this book offers wisdom, encouragement, and hope for the journey ahead.

HOPE FOR THE JOURNEY

God's Design for Marriage is thorough and deeply rooted in the hope you have to see your marriage and relationships flourish and thrive. Holding onto hope as you seek to nurture and strengthen your marriage is what enables it to thrive and flourish amidst life's challenges and joys. This is crucial for the motivation needed to navigate the ups and downs of healing wounds, instilling confidence, and finding the courage to commit to overcoming obstacles—turning them into opportunities to grow deeper in love year after year.

Here's a peek at what your hope can do for you:

1. *Transformation:* Your hope can spark real change in your marriage, bringing you closer to God and each other. By putting the principles in this book into action, you'll see how your relationship can grow in beautiful ways.
2. *Renewed commitment:* This hope will help renew your commitment to each other and to your marriage vows. It is a reminder of the sacredness of the bond you share.
3. *Healing:* When facing challenges or wounds in your relationship, your hope will be a source of healing, reconciliation, and restoration.
4. *Strengthened faith:* Your hope will deepen your faith in God and trust in His plan for your marriage, giving you strength and hope in His promises.
5. *Empowerment:* Your hope will be empowered and equipped with practical tools and strategies to navigate the ups and downs of married life with grace, wisdom, and resilience.
6. *Unity and intimacy:* This hope will empower greater unity and intimacy in your relationship, encouraging deeper emotional, physical, and spiritual connection with each other.
7. *Joy and fulfillment:* Ultimately, your hope will experience the joy and fulfillment that comes from living out God's design for marriage—a love that is sacrificial, unconditional, and enduring.

As you read, complete the Practical Exercises and journal your responses to the Reflection Questions at the end of each chapter.

May you be inspired and encouraged to…

- Embrace your story. It is uniquely yours.
- Align your relationships with Christ. He is the way, the truth, and the life.

- Begin a journey of growth, healing, and spiritual enrichment to love well.
- Be characterized by enduring love, unwavering commitment, and profound unity.
- Shine as a beacon of God's love and grace to the world.
- May this book serve as a guiding light on your journey toward a marriage that is truly by God's design.

CHAPTER ONE

FORGIVENESS AND GRACE

"Be kind to one another, tenderhearted, forgiving one another, as God in Christ forgave you."

~ Ephesians 4:32 (ESV)

In the sacred covenant of marriage, forgiveness, and grace are the foundations that allow love and unity to flourish. When couples give room for forgiveness and grace, they open the door to healing, reconciliation, and growth. It's not just about letting go; it's about restoring the bond you share and moving forward with a renewed sense of connection.

Forgiveness brings healing.

Forgiveness brings restoration, reconciliation, and renewal.

Understanding the power of forgiveness in marriage is essential when facing the inevitable conflicts and challenges that arise. It's not merely a transactional act but a deep spiritual discipline that releases the burdens of resentment and bitterness. This, in turn, opens the door to healing and restoration. In Matthew 6:14-15, Jesus teaches us, *"For if you forgive other people when they sin against you, your heavenly Father will also forgive you. But if you do not forgive others their sins, your Father will not forgive your sins"* (NIV). Through forgiveness, you experience the freedom and grace that come from extending mercy to one another.

Forgiveness brings freedom.

There was a time when I felt the Holy Spirit nudge me to seek forgiveness from my husband. He had just said something to which I took offense. I sat there stewing over it. While justifying my anger and before I said one word, the Holy Spirit reminded me of how forgiveness brings freedom. This was not about my husband but about me. My mind could justify my actions, but my heart had no peace. This was more about the peace that was waiting for me on the other side of obedience.

The peace for which I was desperate.

Realizing that letting go of the offense and giving it to God allowed Him to do mighty work in both of us. We stopped doing the dance of being right. There was very little bantering back and forth but a peaceful silence of healing within our hearts. Forgiveness is knowing that a loving God forgives you when you are not deserving. Jesus paid the price for you to walk in freedom. Sacrificing your will to be a catalyst for positive change in your marriage facilitates the ability to leave the past in the past and live a life you love together. God does not keep a scorecard but keeps a written love letter to you in His Word. Let go and let God be God in your precious life. Just forgive and watch how God shows up to help you to be more than you ever imagined.

God sees you and celebrates you in every moment you choose to move forward on His path for your marriage!

Extending grace and mercy to one another is a foundational aspect of marital love and commitment. Grace recognizes that we are all imperfect beings in need of God's mercy and forgiveness, and it calls us to extend the same compassion and understanding to our spouses. In Colossians 3:13, you are reminded to *"Bear with each other and forgive one another if any of you has a grievance against someone. Forgive as the Lord forgave you"* (NIV). By embracing grace, you create a culture of empathy, humility, and unconditional love within your marriage.

This would be an excellent place to take a moment to look at the meanings of forgiveness, grace, mercy, guilt, and shame.

- *Forgiveness* is the act of pardoning someone for a wrongdoing or offense. In Christianity, forgiveness is central to reconciliation with God and others. It reflects God's forgiveness of our sins through Jesus Christ. It calls us to extend forgiveness to others as we have been forgiven (Ephesians 4:32).
- *Grace* is God's unmerited favor and blessing freely given to humanity. It is a gift from God that we do not deserve but receive through faith in Jesus Christ. Grace enables us to be forgiven, reconciled to God, and empowered to live according to His will (Ephesians 2:8-9).
- *Mercy* is God's compassion and forgiveness shown towards sinners and those in need. It is the withholding of deserved punishment, demonstrating God's loving kindness and willingness to forgive our sins (Ephesians 2:4-5).
- *Guilt* is the awareness of having done wrong or committed sin. In Christian belief, guilt is a result of breaking God's moral laws and brings a sense of responsibility and conviction of sin. Through repentance and receiving God's forgiveness, guilt can be cleansed and replaced with peace and reconciliation (1 John 1:9).
- *Shame* is a painful emotion caused by a sense of guilt, unworthiness, or disgrace. In Christian theology, shame often arises from sin and disobedience to God's will. However, through God's grace and forgiveness, shame can be overcome and replaced with the assurance of His love and acceptance (Romans 10:11).

Often, guilt and shame are interwoven as one. I have found that they are very different. In the book *Father–Daughter Connect*[1] by Marie Louise Rust, she defines guilt as "doing something wrong" and shame as "there is something wrong with me."

These definitions emphasize God's redemptive work through Christ offered to all who believe in Him. Further exploring guilt and shame demonstrates the transformative power of forgiveness, which brings restoration and freedom.

Why embark on a journey of reconciliation, unity, and vision planning with forgiveness as an essential waypoint?

Just as preparing for any journey involves packing your bag with necessities, organizing them for practicality, and ensuring it closes smoothly, so too does preparing emotionally for the journey ahead. Asking simple yet crucial questions—what you truly need, why you need it, and how you can acquire it along the way—ensures a smoother and more enjoyable experience.

However, these questions may stir anxiety, prompting a deeper exploration of what is truly essential versus what may be excess baggage. Emotional baggage, like physical luggage, holds both necessary and unnecessary items. It's crucial to scrutinize and lighten this load before setting out on the journey. As someone who observes people closely, particularly their luggage during travels, I've noticed how some carry-ons are well-worn, barely holding together, while others are pristine and ready for the adventures ahead.

Before heading out on your journey, take a moment to let go of what no longer serves you.

Seek God's guidance on what to carry forward, for He understands the layers of forgiveness and knows when you're ready to shed the next. Forgiveness is the key that unlocks healing, leading to freedom—a freedom that allows you to leave the burdens of the past behind.

When you seek God's forgiveness, He pardons and grants you true deliverance to move forward with joy. I have included a *"Forgiveness Prayer,"*[2] which can be found in the back of the book in the Resource section, which I personally use and recommend to others. I've witnessed miraculous healing through this prayer, as it provides a safe space to acknowledge your pain before God.

Consider this Scripture:

"I urge, then, first of all, that petitions, prayers, intercession and thanksgiving be made for all people—for kings and all those in authority, that we may live peaceful and quiet lives in all godliness and holiness" (1 Timothy 2:1-2 NIV).

A Christian intercessor is someone who mediates on behalf of others in prayer before God. They act as a bridge between individuals or groups and God, bringing their needs, concerns, and petitions before Him. Intercessors typically have a deep commitment to prayer and faith, and they believe in the power of prayer to bring about spiritual and practical change. They often pray for others' healing, guidance, protection, and spiritual growth, aiming to align their prayers with God's will and purposes. Intercessors play a crucial role in Christian communities by interceding for individuals, families, churches, and broader societal needs.

"I have posted watchmen on your walls, Jerusalem; they will never be silent day or night. You who call on the Lord, give yourselves no rest" (Isaiah 62:6 NIV).

An intercessor has been given a gift to hear from God for others as they stand in the gap for another's healing. I often advise my clients that after "*The Forgiveness Prayer,*"[3] they should seek someone who will pray for them as they may experience emotional sensitivity, which is a part of God's healing process in their hearts.

In May of 2007, while standing on the ancient wall of Jerusalem, I received a divine commission as a watchman, experiencing the profound presence of God as His Words resonated within me. This experience reinforced the importance of seeking out someone anointed to intercede on your behalf, a recommendation I often share with new clients.

Forgiveness can be an overwhelming but pivotal part of your journey, initiating profound joy as you embrace it. Initially, it might seem like a daunting risk, and the idea of surrendering to past hurts can feel almost unbearable. However, in reality, it's about surrendering to the healing grace extended by a loving God who promises limitless restoration for your soul—your mind, will, and emotions. Surrendering your thoughts to God's wisdom, aligning your will with His divine purpose, and allowing Him to heal your emotional wounds are central to nurturing Christ-centered marriages and relationships.

Healing beyond your hurts and reconstructing trust in your marriage and relationships is a journey that requires patience, courage, and a willingness to extend grace to one another. The history and time invested in building a relationship can be gradually chipped away with each act of your unforgiveness. Whether you're dealing with betrayal, conflict, or resentment, it's essential to confront past wounds with honesty and humility, seeking God's healing and restoration. Emotions can be unreliable in these moments, influenced by the ebb and flow of past hurts.

In Isaiah 43:18-19, God promises, *"Forget the former things; do not dwell on the past. See, I am doing a new thing! Now it springs up; do you not perceive it? I am making a way in the wilderness and streams in the wasteland"* (NIV). This verse speaks right to the heart of the matter. Forgiveness is not a choice. It is a decree to forgive and to be forgiven.

It is imperative to see yourself as an overcomer, not a victim, if you want to have the marriage and relationships you've always hoped for. Overcoming obstacles that hinder God's intended design for your marriage marks a new path forward—a journey of leaving behind past hurts and surrendering control to God. He alone is perfect in justice and righteousness, always vigilant and ready to bring healing. Rest in His care, pour out your heart to Him, and trust His ability to heal your wounds. Just as physical wounds heal with time, so does emotional healing begin when you entrust your pain to Him.

Through His grace, you find hope and renewal as you journey toward healing and reconciliation. This makes my heart sing! God does what He says He will do for you! He is faithful; therefore, you can be confident because He has never failed on a promise yet and never will.

As we explore forgiveness and grace in marriage, be inspired by God's unfailing love and mercy, and extend the same compassion and grace to one another in your relationships. Embrace the life-changing power of forgiveness and grace, and experience healing, reconciliation, and renewed intimacy within the sacred covenant of marriage.

UNDERSTANDING THE POWER OF FORGIVENESS IN MARRIAGE

Forgiveness is central to a thriving marriage.

Let's look at what it does:

Forgiveness allows you as a couple to heal from hurts and conflicts that naturally arise in any relationship, facilitates emotional healing and reconciliation, and restores harmony and unity.

Forgiveness is essential for rebuilding trust when it has been damaged. It shows a willingness to move past mistakes and rebuild the foundation of trust that is vital for intimacy and mutual respect.

Inevitably, as a couple, you will face disagreements and conflicts. Forgiveness enables you to resolve these conflicts constructively without harboring resentment or holding onto grudges.

Holding onto unforgiveness can lead to bitterness, anger, and emotional distance within the marriage. Forgiveness releases these negative emotions, fostering emotional well-being and promoting a healthier emotional environment.

Forgiveness aligns with teachings about grace, mercy, and love for your spiritual foundation. It reflects God's forgiveness towards you and encourages spiritual growth as an individual and as a couple.

Forgiveness promotes openness and vulnerability in your marriage. It allows you to connect heart to heart to share what matters to you without fear of judgment or rejection, thereby deepening intimacy and connection.

Overall, forgiveness in marriage is crucial because it promotes healing, builds trust, resolves conflicts, enhances emotional well-being, encourages spiritual growth, and strengthens your bond, creating a foundation for a thriving and enduring relationship based on love, grace, and mutual respect.

For this to be effective, healthy boundaries need to be put into place. Your relationship is to be balanced between the give and take of a growing and thriving marriage. Some days, it looks like 80/20. Others say it may look like 20/80. Each spouse needs to try to give their best 100% on any given day together.

Boundaries around forgiveness involve setting expectations for how forgiveness is sought and granted, ensuring that it is a genuine process of healing rather than a superficial gesture.

This includes boundaries around sincerely apologizing, acknowledging hurt without minimizing it, and committing to working through the underlying issues that led to the need for forgiveness. Such boundaries protect the integrity of the forgiveness process and prevent resentment from lingering, allowing grace to abound in the marriage.

To be a catalyst for healthy boundaries through forgiveness, start with clear apologies. It's important to carefully point out what you're apologizing for, like saying, "I'm sorry for _____. Would you please forgive me?" This shows genuine remorse. You can also ask, "What can I do to help us reconcile?" But ideally, you have to be the change you want in your relationship.

Next, embrace the forgiveness process by agreeing on boundaries, including time to heal, discussing expectations for change, and not bringing up past forgiven offenses in future conflicts.

Finally, commit to supporting each other. Offer grace and support to each other in moments of weakness or mistakes, and remember that forgiveness is a continuous process that requires patience and understanding.

There is a biblical understanding of the power of forgiveness in marriage, and it is rooted in the very heart of God's redemptive plan for humanity. Throughout Scripture, forgiveness is portrayed as a central theme in God's relationship with His people, and it serves as a model for the forgiveness that spouses are called to extend to one another within the marital relationship.

When the Apostle Paul urges believers to *"Be kind to one another, tenderhearted, forgiving one another, as God in Christ forgave you"* (Ephesians 4:32 ESV), it encapsulates the essence of biblical forgiveness – rooted in God's boundless love and mercy, compassion, and grace extended not only to others but also to you.

The power of forgiveness lies in its ability to release the burdens of resentment, bitterness, and anger that can poison marital relationships. When you choose to forgive another, you choose to let go of past wrongs and hurts and open the door wide for healing, reconciliation, and restoration. In that moment, you make a powerful decision to release the person or memory to God, allowing yourself the freedom to heal. It is at that moment when you are able to let go and let God be God.

In Colossians 3:13, Paul encourages believers to *"Bear with each other and forgive one another if any of you has a grievance against someone. Forgive as the Lord forgave you"* (NIV). This verse reveals the Holy Spirit's power of forgiveness for unity, reconciliation, and love within the marital relationship. Some hurt feels too powerful, making forgiveness unattainable, but within you, there is a resurrection power when you are in Christ!

In the journey of forgiveness and grace within marriage, establishing healthy boundaries is essential for healing and restoration. Forgiveness is not merely a one-time act but a deliberate choice to release oneself from the emotional bondage of bitterness and resentment. Setting boundaries around forgiveness allows you to reclaim your emotional well-being and spiritual freedom.

When you choose to forgive, you are not necessarily absolving the other person of responsibility or even communicating forgiveness directly to them. Instead, forgiveness is primarily an internal decision, a personal choice to release the grip of hurt and anger. This inner healing process is crucial because it liberates the forgiver from carrying the weight of past grievances, allowing you to move forward with renewed hope and peace.

Healthy boundaries in forgiveness also involve setting limits on how much emotional energy and thought are dedicated to past hurts. It means consciously choosing not to dwell on grievances or replaying painful memories. By redirecting your focus toward personal growth, spiritual renewal, and cultivating a deeper connection with God, you can break free from the cycle of resentment.

Moreover, forgiveness opens the door to grace—a divine gift that brings healing and reconciliation. By extending grace to yourself and others, you are embracing God's mercy and love. This will not only strengthen your togetherness but also dismantle the stronghold of bitterness, paving the way for God's healing work to mend broken relationships.

In the context of marriage, establishing these boundaries around forgiveness and grace encourages an environment where both of you can grow spiritually and emotionally. It allows for genuine reconciliation and renewal of trust, creating a foundation built on God's design of love and forgiveness.

Biblical understanding of forgiveness in marriage is grounded in the example of Christ Himself. In His earthly ministry, Jesus demonstrated the power of forgiveness through His words and actions, offering forgiveness to sinners, outcasts, and even those who crucified Him.

In Luke 23:34, as Jesus hung on the cross, He prayed, *"Father, forgive them, for they do not know what they are doing"* (NIV). This radical act of forgiveness exemplifies the sacrificial love and grace that spouses are called to emulate within their own marriages.

Ultimately, the biblical understanding of the power of forgiveness in marriage is rooted in the transformative work of God's grace. God offers us the gift of redemption and reconciliation through His forgiveness, and He calls us to extend that same grace to one another within the marital relationship. As you forgive one another, you participate in God's redemptive work, experiencing healing, restoration, and renewed intimacy within your marriage.

EXTENDING GRACE AND MERCY TO ONE ANOTHER

In the Bible, "grace" refers to the unmerited favor and kindness shown by God toward humanity, particularly in the form of salvation through Jesus Christ. It is a gift freely given, not earned by human effort. "Mercy," on the other hand, is compassion or forgiveness shown to someone who deserves punishment or judgment. It involves withholding deserved consequences and offering forgiveness or relief instead.

The importance of extending grace and mercy to one another cannot be overstated when it comes to building the marriage you've dreamed of having. In the sacred covenant of marriage, grace and mercy serve as essential ingredients for fostering love, unity, and lasting fulfillment.

Extending grace and mercy to one another means showing kindness, compassion, and understanding, even in the face of imperfections, mistakes, and shortcomings. It involves choosing to overlook offenses, forgive past hurts, and give each other the benefit of the doubt, just as God has shown us grace and mercy in our own lives.

When you extend grace and mercy to one another, you create a culture of acceptance, forgiveness, and unconditional love within your marriage. Instead of holding onto grudges or harboring resentment, you choose to approach each other with humility, empathy, and a willingness to reconcile.

> *When you extend grace and mercy to one another, you create a culture of acceptance, forgiveness, and unconditional love within your marriage.*

Extending grace and mercy to one another cultivates a spirit of unity and partnership within your marital relationship. Instead of viewing each other through a lens of judgment or criticism, spouses choose to see each other through the eyes of love and grace, recognizing each other's inherent worth and value as beloved children of God.

Ultimately, the importance of extending grace and mercy to one another lies in its matchless power to heal, restore, and strengthen the marital bond. As you embrace the importance of extending grace and mercy to your spouse, you are prepared for a journey of growth, healing, and transformation that leads to the marriage you have dreamed of having – one marked by love, unity, and the abundant blessings of God's grace.

HEALING PAST HURTS AND REBUILDING TRUST

Healing past hurts and rebuilding trust is a crucial aspect of encouraging a healthy and thriving marriage. In your marital relationship, there may be instances of pain, betrayal, or disappointment that have left wounds in the hearts of both of you. However, by addressing these hurts with honesty, humility, and a commitment to healing, you can overcome past traumas and rebuild trust, laying a foundation for a stronger and more resilient marriage.

Healing past hurts begins with acknowledging and validating each other's feelings and experiences. By listening to each other with empathy and compassion, you can begin the process of healing old wounds and moving forward together.

Moreover, healing past hurts involves forgiveness – both seeking forgiveness from one another for past wrongs and extending forgiveness for hurts inflicted. Forgiveness is not about condoning or excusing harmful behavior but about releasing the hold that past hurts have on the marital relationship. In Matthew 6:14-15, Jesus teaches, *"For if you forgive others their trespasses, your heavenly Father will also forgive you, but if you do not forgive others their trespasses, neither will your Father forgive your trespasses"* (ESV). By choosing to forgive one another, you open the door to healing, reconciliation, and restoration.

Rebuilding trust is a gradual process that requires time, patience, and consistent effort. It involves being trustworthy and reliable in word and deed, demonstrating integrity, transparency, and honesty in all interactions. Trust is built through small acts of kindness, consistency, and follow-through as you both demonstrate your commitment to each other's well-being and the health of the marriage.

Ultimately, healing past hurts and rebuilding trust is a journey that requires mutual commitment, understanding, and grace. It is a process of growth and transformation that leads to deeper intimacy, connection, and resilience within the marital relationship. As you work together to heal old wounds and rebuild trust, you lay a foundation for a marriage characterized by love, mutual respect, and unwavering trust.

Forgiveness brings healing, and grace helps you to be the person God created you to be and to have the marriage He designed for you to have, walking it out in everyday life together. Matthew 6:14 reminds us, *"For if you forgive other people when they sin against you, your heavenly Father will also forgive you"* (NIV). You need to forgive to be forgiven. As my husband and I agree that "neither one of us is perfect, but we are perfect together."

Remember that forgiveness is not just a singular act but an ongoing process of grace and healing in your marriage. By embracing forgiveness, you pave the way for deeper understanding, empathy, and resilience. It sets the stage for the next chapter in your marital journey—the blueprint for building a Christ-centered union that reflects God's design for marriage.

May you find forgiveness as the first step for healing.

Practical Exercises

Which of the following practical exercises are you ready to commit to? Please check the appropriate box.

- ♡ Set aside dedicated time to reflect on past conflicts or grievances within your relationship. Pick one past conflict or grievance and practice forgiveness by expressing empathy, understanding, and a willingness to let go of resentment or anger.

- ♡ Practice acts of kindness and generosity toward your spouse, even in moments of tension or disagreement. Look for opportunities to extend grace and mercy, choosing compassion and understanding over judgment or criticism.

- ♡ Explore opportunities for professional counseling or therapy to address deeper issues of trust and forgiveness within your relationship. Seek support from a trained Christian therapist or counselor who can provide guidance and tools for healing and reconciliation.

How do you plan to accomplish your selected option?

_____
_____
_____
_____

Can you explain why you chose this particular option?

_____
_____
_____
_____

Reflection Questions

What barriers or obstacles prevent you from fully embracing forgiveness in your relationship?

_____
_____
_____
_____
_____

How can you cultivate a spirit of forgiveness and reconciliation in your marriage?

_____
_____
_____
_____
_____

In what areas do you struggle to extend grace and mercy in your relationship?

_____
_____
_____
_____
_____

By now, you've probably realized that change begins with you. You can't change someone else, but you can be a catalyst for healthy change in your marriage and relationships. Take the opportunity to be that change by letting go and giving God every grievance, hurt, and lie, especially changing your heart to be healed by His love. Remember, forgiveness is the best gift you can give yourself. This is your life to live in the freedom that only Christ offers.

When you engage in these practical exercises and reflection questions, you can deepen your understanding of forgiveness and grace in marriage and take tangible steps toward healing and reconciliation. You can cultivate a relationship built on trust, love, and grace through empathy, compassion, and a commitment to forgiveness.

CHAPTER TWO

FOUNDATIONS OF FAITH – GOD'S BLUEPRINT FOR MARRIAGE

"Therefore a man shall leave his father and his mother and hold fast to his wife, and they shall become one flesh."

~ Genesis 2:24 (ESV)

*B*efore you begin to build a Christ-centered marriage, you will need a blueprint to build a strong foundation. Just as you would plan meticulously with each detail of a dream destination to get the most out of your time together, you also want to be sure you are going to have a clear direction to have the best life together. Knowing your destination and the path to get there is foundational, wouldn't you agree?

For your marriage to withstand the test of time and circumstances, this blueprint is not merely a set of rules but a divine blueprint for cultivating love, respect, and unity in alignment with God's perfect will. Together, you will discover how to build a marriage that honors God and fulfills His purpose, setting a course for lasting joy and fulfillment.

Let's start at the beginning with creation as God's blueprint for marriage.

As the crowning jewels of God's creation, Adam and Eve were entrusted with the privilege and responsibility of stewarding the earth and cultivating a relationship with their Creator.

God's design for marriage is evident in His creation of Eve as a suitable partner and companion for Adam. From the beginning, God intended for Adam and Eve to experience unity, intimacy, and mutual love within their marital relationship. Their union was founded on a deep sense of purpose and shared responsibility as they worked together to fulfill God's command to be fruitful, multiply, and fill the earth.

Despite the challenges they faced, including the temptation and subsequent fall into sin, Adam and Eve's story serves as a powerful reminder of the importance of faith in God and in their union, known as marriage. A relationship with God was central to their identity and purpose, providing them with the strength and guidance they needed to navigate the complexities together.

Your relationship with God is of great importance and central to your identity and purpose. Gather your thoughts, reflect on your faith, and take this moment to ask God for His strength and guidance so that you can go further into navigating life together with all its ebbs and flows. This is your moment to ask. Don't let this moment pass you by without bringing your marriage before the One who created you in His image, providing you with a life in unity with Him, your spouse, and others.

Understanding God's blueprint for marriage is fundamental to building a relationship that truly reflects His divine intention. As we go deeper into this, you will explore the timeless principles and truths that underpin a Christ–centered marriage. The following three principles are guiding points that serve as a compass, taking you through the complexities of life together, emphasizing unity, love, and the mutual commitment to honor God in your union.

By aligning with God's design, you will discover the profound joy and enduring strength that come from living out His blueprint for marriage. This alignment is not just a path to joy but also a source of strength that can sustain you through life's challenges.

Let's take a look at God's blueprint for marriage.

GOD'S ORIGIN OF MARRIAGE

The origins of marriage, as outlined in the Bible, are rooted in the creation story found in the book of Genesis, the book of "beginnings." The story begins with the creation of the first man, Adam, whom God formed from the dust of the ground. Genesis 2:18-25 gives insight into the creation of Eve and the establishment of marriage as a foundational institution of human society.

Let us take a moment to imagine the beginning of creation — a time with power, beauty, and perfect alignment with God's spoken Word. The sound, the harmony, and the silent pauses reflect the creation of all things good from the hand of God.

You may see Michelangelo's "*Creation Of Adam*" painting of God's hand reaching for Adam's.[4] Or hear a Heaven–inspired Overture "*I Am*"[5] that speaks to your heart. God's Words transcend all human experience, and this is what He has in store for you as His child. To go higher and aim higher with Him is to receive from His heart your precious heart. As His child through salvation found in Christ alone, you have access to a storehouse of treasures, all found in knowing and trusting His limitless love for a life of faith. This suggests that as a believer, you have access to God's abundant spiritual blessings and resources simply by understanding and relying on His limitless provisions to live out your faith.

God recognized that it was not good for Adam to be alone, so He created Eve as a suitable helper and companion for him. Upon seeing Eve for the first time, Adam's response is one of profound recognition and connection. He declares, *"This is now bone of my bones and flesh of my flesh; she shall be called Woman because she was taken out of Man"* (Genesis 2:23 KJV). This expression of unity and intimacy between Adam and Eve is a foundational example of God's design for marriage. Adam and Eve's relationship embodies the essence of God's blueprint for marriage—a partnership marked by unity, companionship, and mutual support.

From the beginning, marriage was intended to be a sacred union between one man and one woman, reflecting God's image and intended to fulfill His purposes on earth. By exploring the origins of marriage in the creation narrative of Adam and Eve, we gain valuable insights into the sacredness and significance of marriage as a divine institution ordained by God—Himself.

As you seek to build Christ-centered marriages and relationships, you can draw inspiration from the timeless truths in the story of Adam and Eve. Adopt God's design for your marriage and experience the blessings that come from walking in obedience to His will.

GOD'S PURPOSE OF MARRIAGE

The purpose of marriage is multifaceted, encompassing companionship, procreation, and mutual support. This highlights the role of marriage in the continuation of the human race through procreation. Additionally, marriage provides a context for companionship, emotional support, and partnership in fulfilling God's purpose for individuals and families.

The Bible provides profound insights into the purpose of marriage, encompassing both the Old and New Testaments. Here is what Scripture reveals about the purpose of marriage, including references from the New Testament.

In Genesis 2:18, God declares, *"It is not good that the man should be alone; I will make him a helper fit for him"* (ESV). One of the primary purposes of marriage is to provide companionship and support for one another. Marriage offers the opportunity for you to journey through life together, sharing joys, burdens, and experiences in a partnership marked by love and mutual care.

Genesis 1:28: *"And God blessed them, and God said unto them, Be fruitful, and multiply, and replenish the earth, and subdue it"* (KJV). Marriage's role is for procreation and the formation of families. Through marriage, you have the privilege and responsibility of raising godly children, nurturing them in a loving and stable environment, and passing on faith and values from generation to generation.

Ephesians 5:31-32 highlights the mystery of marriage, comparing it to the union between Christ and the Church. The Apostle Paul writes, *"Therefore a man shall leave his father and mother and hold fast to his wife, and the two shall become one flesh"* (ESV). This passage underscores the unity and oneness that marriage brings, both spiritually and physically, as both of you are joined together in a covenant relationship. This unity is a powerful bond that can bring you closer together in your marriage.

Marriage provides a framework for spiritual growth and partnership in serving God. 1 Corinthians 7:14 (ESV) speaks to the sanctifying influence that believers can have on their unbelieving spouses as they walk together in faith. Additionally, you are called to support and encourage one another in your spiritual journey, praying together, studying God's Word, and serving Him faithfully as a team.

Ephesians 5:25-33 (NLT) instructs husbands to love their wives sacrificially, as Christ loved the church, and wives to respect and submit to their husbands. This Scripture underscores the sincere symbolism of marriage, reflecting the selfless love and unity exemplified in the relationship between Christ and His bride, the Church. By living out these roles in marriage, you bear witness to the transformative power of Christ's love in their relationship.

The origin, intent, and purpose of marriage, as outlined in the Bible, encompasses companionship, procreation, unity, spiritual growth, and reflecting Christ's love. By embracing these purposes and aligning your marriage with God's design, you can experience the fullness of blessings and fulfillment that come from walking in obedience to His will. God's blessings are incorporated within His design for your marriage.

SIGNIFICANCE IN GOD'S DESIGN FOR MARRIAGE

Marriage significantly impacts God's plan for humanity. Ephesians 5:31-32 (KJV) compares the marital relationship to the union between Christ and the Church, emphasizing the unfailing mystery of Christ's love for His people. As husbands and wives love and submit to one another, they reflect the sacrificial love and unity exemplified in the relationship between Christ and His Church. Additionally, marriage serves as a foundational institution for raising godly offspring and passing on faith from generation to generation.

I heard my biological clock ticking. I was beginning to lose hope of finding that special someone. Although I was excited about my career choice, I found myself praying for more than a career. My faith brought me to a place of not seeking "why" I was still single but to a place of "how" I will live my life with God.

I found myself praying for my husband before I knew of him. I had not even dreamed of a wedding or a future with someone. The only dream I had was opening a florist shop and greenhouse one day. There had been disappointments in my life, but I still had hope that one day, all of it would change.

So, I prayed. There was a constant nudging to pray. I had known Jesus my whole life and heard about all the possibilities of living a life pleasing to Him. I wanted that, too.

Everything changed when I was offered a job in a plant nursery and greenhouse for a landscaping company. I took the job, and that was where I met my husband. There were no sparks or connections, but when I look back, I remember being in the right place at the right time. Strangely enough, he felt familiar.

It all happened fast. Suddenly, my heart was connected to his, my prayers were being answered, and the day came when I walked down the aisle of the church I had known since I was a young girl. This is where I first fell in love with Jesus, and now, the man of my dreams is waiting for me at the altar.

This was never about me or him but something much bigger. God knew it all along! He prepared me to trust again, to leave all the disappointment behind, and put my hand in the hand of the man who saw and pursued me. Faith makes a way when there is no way. Every step with faith keeps you on the right path to where love, faith, and commitment meet each other at the right time.

You see, the significance of God's blueprint for marriage is profound and far-reaching, impacting not just you but those around you, as well as your family and society as a whole. God knew you before He created the world, long before you were being knitted together with His plan and purpose for your life. Even as you were being formed in your mother's womb, He already knew the purpose of your marriage.

Marriage reflects the image of God in humanity. Genesis 1:27 states, *"So God created mankind in his own image, in the image of God he created them; male and female he created them"* (NIV). The union of a man and a woman in marriage mirrors the relational nature of the triune God—Father, Son, and Holy Spirit—and reflects His love, unity, and creativity.

God's purpose for marriage is to provide a stable foundation for families. Healthy marriages contribute to the well-being and stability of children, providing them with love, security, and guidance as they grow and develop. Strong families, in turn, form the building blocks of healthy societies, fostering stability, social cohesion, and flourishing communities.

Spiritual growth and partnership in serving God and each other also serve as a framework for marriage. You support and encourage one another in your faith journey, praying together, studying God's Word, and serving Him faithfully as a team. Through the challenges and joys of marriage, individuals have the opportunity to gain experience in their relationship with God and with each other.

Marriage bears witness to the life–changing power of Christ's love in human relationships. Ephesians 5:25-27 (ESV) describes Christ's sacrificial love for His bride, the Church, and calls husbands to love their wives in the same way. By living out these roles in marriage, you reflect the selfless love, unity, and commitment exemplified in the relationship between Christ and His Church.

A Christ–centered marriage is a powerful witness to the world. When you honor God in your relationship, you demonstrate the beauty, joy, and fulfillment that come from walking in obedience to His will. Your love and commitment shine as a light in a world that often struggles with brokenness and despair, pointing others to the transformative power of God's love.

The significance of God's plan for marriage lies in its reflection of His image, its role in building strong families and societies, its potential for spiritual growth and partnership, its reflection of Christ's love, and its witness to the world. By embracing God's design for marriage, you can experience the fullness of blessings and fulfillment that come from aligning your marriage and relationships with His purpose.

Christ–centered relationships, rooted in the timeless wisdom of Scripture, focus on understanding the biblical framework that guides and shapes a marriage according to God's design. Grab your journal as you explore key passages illuminating the essence of Christ–centered relationships shedding light on the roles, responsibilities, and dynamics that characterize such unions. Take note of these things.

Meditate on these things in your heart. Surrender your thoughts as you seek to replace them with God's wisdom on their impact on your relationship.

Rest assured, He will answer you lovingly and with respect.

The significance of aligning your relationships with the teachings of Christ is to draw inspiration from His example of love, sacrifice, and servanthood. You lay a solid foundation for marriage that honors God and reflects His glory by grounding your marriage and relationships in biblical truth.

I found that when I align myself with God's purpose for my life, I feel confident that I am on the right path by listening for the small, still voice I receive from reading the Word of God. This assured me that not only would I have the marriage that God had for me, but I would also be aligned with the man God had for me. To know God is to know His Word. When you know God's Word, you have His promises. He has not failed on one promise yet. Keep in mind that God's promises are found when you follow His path.

The need for God's blueprint for marriage as a sacred covenant between a man and a woman is accentuated by its portrayal as a union of oneness, a reflection of Christ's relationship with the Church, and a divine institution ordained by God—Himself.

This blueprint provides a clear framework for understanding your roles and responsibilities within the marriage. It encourages you to cultivate a togetherness rooted in love, respect, and mutual support. By holding onto these divine principles, you can navigate the complexities of life together, drawing strength from your faith and deepening your emotional and spiritual connection.

By honoring the sacredness of marriage and embracing its covenantal nature, you can experience the blessings and fulfillment that come from walking in obedience to God's design.

How can you navigate your journey without a plan? Whether running errands or heading out on a trip, having a clear plan guides you toward reaching your destination.

Understanding your personal and marital purpose directs you on the path God intends for you to follow.

One of my favorite exercises that has lasting effects is helping others to create a vision for their life and marriage. It provides direction and clarity, like charting a course toward your dreams and goals as a blueprint for the future. It is not just about setting goals once; it's an ongoing process of refining and adapting as you journey through different seasons of life.

What excites me most is that this practice helps you stay focused and motivated and strengthens your marriage by aligning your priorities and aspirations with God's plan. If you revisit and adjust your vision, you'll find new inspiration and purpose, deepening your commitment to each other and God's design for your marriage.

Keep in mind that creating a vision is more than just a practical exercise—it is a powerful tool that aligns your relationship with His design. In today's world, where biblical marriages face increasing challenges, having a clear vision rooted in God's will is crucial.

A vision for your marriage serves as a tangible expression of your shared dreams, goals, and aspirations as a couple. It provides a visual representation of the future you envision together, rooted in God's purpose for your lives.

Here is why having a vision is essential:

Creating a vision clarifies what you both desire for your marriage. It helps articulate your individual and collective goals, whether they relate to spiritual growth, family, career, or personal development. This clarity fosters unity and strengthens your commitment to pursuing God's will together.

> *A vision for your marriage serves as a tangible expression of your shared dreams, goals, and aspirations as a couple.*

By intentionally seeking God's guidance and aligning your aspirations with His Word, a vision becomes a tool for discerning His purpose for your marriage. It allows you to prayerfully consider and incorporate biblical principles into your shared vision, ensuring that your goals honor God and contribute to His kingdom.

Visualizing your dreams and goals can be highly motivating. A vision serves as a constant reminder of what you are working towards as a couple. It encourages perseverance during challenges and celebrates milestones as you progress toward your shared vision.

Building a vision together nurtures open communication and collaboration. It encourages meaningful discussions about your values, priorities, and dreams. Through this process, you deepen your understanding of each other's hearts and strengthen your emotional connection.

Once created, a written vision serves as a commitment to each other and God. It holds you accountable to the goals and values you have set as a couple, promoting a sense of responsibility and mutual support in achieving them.

A written vision is not merely a collage of images and words—it is a sacred space where you invite God's presence into your marriage journey. It helps you navigate challenges with faith, celebrate victories with gratitude, and continuously align your lives with God's perfect plan for your relationship.

Another way of creating a vision is to put images on a poster board or something similar to what you do together. Often, this becomes an enjoyable experience that you display to be reminded on a daily basis of your commitment to your future.

By identifying and articulating your marriage's purpose on a vision board, you invite God into the center of your relationship. This act of intentional vision-setting helps you see the bigger picture of your marriage, guiding you to glorify God's kingdom and live in the freedom He offers through His Spirit. You will find a step-by-step guide (**VISION PLANNING FOR YOUR MARRIAGE**) in the Resource section at the back of this workbook.

Practical Exercises

♡ Create a vision board individually and then as a couple, illustrating your shared goals and aspirations for your marriage. (Instructions for **VISION PLANNING FOR YOUR MARRIAGE** can be found in the Resource section at the back of this workbook.)

How will you commit to this exercise and actively collaborate to achieve these goals?

_____

_____

_____

_____

_____

_____

_____

_____

_____

_____

_____

_____

_____

_____

Reflection Questions

How does understanding God's blueprint for marriage impact your perspective on your relationship?

_____
_____
_____
_____
_____

What practical steps can you take to align your marriage with God's design?

_____
_____
_____
_____
_____

How can you incorporate the principles of companionship, unity, and spiritual growth into your daily life as a couple?

_____
_____
_____
_____
_____

CHAPTER THREE

UNDERSTANDING GOD'S PLAN FOR MARRIAGE

"For this reason a man will leave his father and mother and be united to his wife, and the two will become one flesh. This is a profound mystery—but I am talking about Christ and the church. However, each one of you also must love his wife as he loves himself, and the wife must respect her husband."

~ Ephesians 5:31–33 (NIV)

God's plan for marriage is rooted in His divine wisdom and purpose. It's not merely a social institution but a sacred covenant ordained by God—Himself. In God's plan, marriage is designed to reflect the unity, love, and commitment found within the Trinity, where two individuals become one flesh in a lifelong partnership.

While God's Blueprint for marriage emphasizes the specific design or structure that He has ordained for marriage, this would include the principle of a lifelong and exclusive sacred covenant between a man and woman, the role of submission and love, and guidelines of faithfulness and purity. Understanding His plan for marriage involves a broader scope, which includes the personal side of how marriages can fulfill and reflect His glory.

Understanding this plan involves embracing the biblical principles of mutual love, respect, and submission, as well as the call to bear fruitfulness and multiply both spiritually and physically. Ultimately, God's plan for marriage is centered on glorifying Him and experiencing the abundant blessings He intends for couples who walk in obedience to His Word.

Throughout this chapter, you will examine each of these four pillars, exploring their biblical significance, practical implications, and transformative power in shaping your marriage that honors God and reflects His divine purpose. You'll journey into the heart of God's design for marriage, where embracing the foundational *Four Pillars of a Biblical Marriage* will serve as the bedrock of marital unity, fulfillment, and joy. (**THE FOUR FOUNDATIONAL PILLARS OF GOD'S PROMISES** can be found in the Resources section at the back of this book.)

EXPLORING BIBLICAL FOUNDATIONS OF MARRIAGE

In the sacred covenant of marriage, God has laid a foundation built upon timeless principles and truths that serve as pillars of strength, unity, and purpose. There are four pillars for biblical marriage: deeply rooted in Scripture, the divine blueprint for marital harmony, fulfillment, and godly living. Notice the rich tapestry of God's Word that uncovers the matchless wisdom and guidance they offer.

THE FOUR PILLARS OF A BIBLICAL MARRIAGE

Pillar 1 - Foundation in Christ

"And whatever you do, in word or deed, do everything in the name of the Lord Jesus, giving thanks to God the Father through him" (Colossians 3:17 ESV).

The first pillar of a biblical marriage is having a strong foundation underscoring the centrality of Christ in marriage. With Christ as the center of your marriage, His teachings, grace, and presence will guide, sustain, and enrich your relationship. You can be assured that, like a strong threefold cord (Ecclesiastes 4:12), your marriage will not easily break. You will never be alone in your joys and struggles.

To help you remember, here is an acronym for how to keep Him as your center:

C ommitment: A Christ-centered marriage prioritizes your commitment to Christ first, which in turn strengthens your commitment. (Ephesians 5:22-33)

H armony: Christ brings harmony to the marriage, aligning your hearts and minds with His will and purpose. (Colossians 3:14-15 ESV)

R espect: Christ's example of love and respect will guide you to honor and value each other's roles and contributions within the marriage. (Ephesians 5:33 NLT)

I ntimacy: Through Christ's love, you can deepen your spiritual experience and emotional intimacy and strengthen your bond and connection. (Song of Solomon 5:16)

S acrifice: Christ's sacrificial love serves as the model for husbands and wives to sacrificially serve and support one another in the marriage. (Ephesians 5:25-28 ESV)

T rust: Trust in Christ will promote trust between the two of you, knowing that Christ is the cornerstone of a healthy, strong foundation, guiding you through challenges through all seasons of life. (Proverbs 3:5-6 KJV)

Building your marriage on Christ means committing to love, respect, and trust each other. When you do this, your relationship truly reflects Christ's love and shows how beautiful God's design for marriage is. Inviting Jesus into your daily life brings His guidance into your home. This approach showcases how His teachings and grace can transform your marriage, making it a shining example of God's love in the world.

It is not merely about acknowledging Jesus as a distant figure in marriage; it's about inviting Him into the very fabric of the relationship. It's about allowing His teachings to permeate every aspect of marital life, from communication and conflict resolution to intimacy and shared goals.

When anchoring your marriage in Christ, bringing Him into every aspect of your life together, draw upon His wisdom, grace, and love to navigate challenges and celebrate joys; remind you that Christ is not just an observer but an active participant in your union, guiding, sustaining, and enriching your journey together.

It's about cultivating a deep, intimate relationship with Christ individually and as a couple. Hence, His presence becomes the cornerstone of your prayer life and marital bond, strengthening you to weather any storm and rejoice in every blessing.

Pillar 2 - Mutual Love and Respect

"Love one another with mutual affection; anticipate one another in showing honor" (Romans 12:10 NABRE).

In the context of marriage, you are to love each other with genuine affection and anticipate each other's needs, showing honor and respect in your interactions. This pillar emphasizes the importance of selfless love, mutual honor, and adoring respect within the marital relationship.

It's about prioritizing each other's well-being, honoring their perspectives and feelings, and cherishing one another deeply. As you navigate life together, remember to embody Christ's sacrificial love and mutual respect, as this strengthens your togetherness and honors God's design for marriage.

Believe your relationship to be a testament to the life-changing power of Christ–centered love and mutual respect in building a lasting and fulfilling marriage.

It also calls believers to a higher standard of love and respect within the Christian community. It's not merely about loving others but loving them with genuine, mutual affection beyond surface–level niceties. Anticipating one another in showing honor implies a proactive attitude of humility and servanthood, where each person seeks to uplift and honor others before themselves.

This verse challenges us to build deep, meaningful relationships characterized by selflessness, kindness, and honor, reflecting the love of Christ in all our interactions.

Pillar 3 - Fruitfulness and Multiplication

"be fruitful and multiply and fill the earth and replenish it" (Genesis 1:28 KJV).

This decree includes the physical bearing of children and the spiritual and relational fruitfulness that marriage can produce. It speaks to your potential to cultivate a legacy of love, faith, and service that extends beyond yourself and impacts future generations.

Just as God commanded Adam and Eve to multiply and fill the earth, you are called to cultivate a legacy of love, faith, and service that extends beyond yourself.

The intentional cultivation of a marriage that not only thrives in the present but also positively impacts future generations. It involves nurturing spiritual growth through shared faith practices and principles, thereby leaving behind a heritage of spiritual strength and influence.

This commitment to relational health fosters a marriage marked by love, respect, and unity, serving as a model for healthy relationships within the family and community. Engaging in acts of service and ministry together further enhances this legacy of compassion and generosity.

By living out God's plan for marriage with integrity and purpose, you can influence children, grandchildren, and beyond, imparting values and principles that reflect God's love and purpose for marriage, thus ensuring a lasting impact for future generations.

Living out God's plan for your marriage involves daily commitment, intentional actions, and reliance on God's grace to navigate challenges and celebrate joys, ultimately glorifying God through the marital union.

It has the potential for your marriage to impact future generations by nurturing strong family bonds, passing down faith traditions, and living out God's purposes together. It's about leaving a lasting legacy of spiritual and relational fruitfulness that reflects God's love and grace to those around them.

Pillar 4 – Unity in Marriage

"Therefore shall a man leave his father and his mother, and shall cleave unto his wife: and they shall be one flesh" (Genesis 2:24 KJV).

Unity in marriage is the foundational pillar emphasizing the profound oneness between husband and wife. This oneness is not merely physical but encompasses the marital bond's spiritual, emotional, and relational aspects.

At its core, unity in marriage reflects the divine intention for two individuals to become one flesh, as outlined in Genesis 2:24 (KJV). This unity is a sacred union that transcends mere companionship, forming the bedrock upon which the entire marital relationship is built.

Unity in marriage involves a deep commitment to each other's well-being, mutual respect, and shared purpose. It requires prioritizing the needs and desires of the marital unit above individual interests, welcoming a sense of teamwork in navigating life's challenges and joys together.

Also, unity in marriage is not static but dynamic, requiring continuous cultivation and nurturing. You must actively invest in your relationship, furthering open communication, trust, and vulnerability to strengthen your unity over time.

Actively investing in your marriage means prioritizing open communication, trust-building, and vulnerability to foster a strong and enduring connection. Regular and honest communication allows you and your spouse to openly share your thoughts, feelings, and aspirations, deepening understanding and intimacy.

Building trust is all about consistency, transparency, and honoring commitments, which lays a solid foundation for mutual respect and reliability. When you embrace vulnerability, it creates a safe space for both partners to share fears and insecurities without judgment, which really strengthens emotional bonds.

Together, these efforts cultivate unity as you navigate life's challenges and celebrate victories, ensuring your marriage thrives with integrity and purpose.

Unity in marriage reflects the divine unity within the Godhead and serves as a powerful testimony to the world of God's love, grace, and faithfulness. Embrace unity in your relationship, experience deeper intimacy, fulfillment, and joy, and reflect the beauty of God's design for marriage.

These four pillars rest on the solid foundation upon which a Christ–centered marriage is built, providing you with a framework for understanding God's design and purpose for marriage and guiding you toward a relationship that reflects your Heavenly Father's love, unity, and grace.

> *Unity in marriage reflects the divine unity within the Godhead and serves as a powerful testimony to the world of God's love, grace, and faithfulness.*

THE ROLES OF HUSBAND AND WIFE ACCORDING TO SCRIPTURE

In the intricate dance of marriage, each partner plays a unique role, contributing to the harmony and stability of the union. Just as a well-choreographed performance requires each dancer to know their steps, a successful marriage thrives on the clarity and understanding of each spouse's role.

But why is it essential to identify these roles?

Exploring the profound significance of defining the roles of husband and wife in marriage clarifies the foundation for unity, balance, mutual respect, effective communication, and spiritual alignment within the marital bond.

These roles are designed not as rigid stereotypes but as complementary expressions of God's intended harmony within marriage, rooted in biblical principles. Scripture provides clear guidance on how husbands are called to sacrificially lead their families with love and humility, mirroring Christ's selfless devotion to the church. Likewise, wives are encouraged to respect and support their husbands, fostering an environment of mutual honor and unity.

Understanding and embracing these roles not only enriches marital dynamics but also reflects God's wisdom and intentionality in creating harmonious and flourishing relationships. At the core of a Christ-centered marital union lies a spiritual power, binding commitment, and nurturing of the strength needed for enduring, healthy marriages.

Now, let's go further into the timeless wisdom of Scripture to study the distinct roles of husbands and wives, essential pillars in building a Christ-centered marriage that withstands the test of time and trials.

Prepare your heart for when faith, love, and commitment meet in the roles of husband and wife.

Roles of the Husband

In the intricate tapestry of marriage, each partner brings unique gifts, responsibilities, and roles to the union. Among these, the role of the husband holds particular significance, rooted in biblical principles and cultural expectations. Although this may not align with prevalent views today, it stands as the opposite of what we will explore. Ultimately, aligning with God's will for marriage brings joy to the Lord's heart.

Prepare your heart for the moment faith, love, and commitment intersect within the roles of husband and wife, aligning with God's heart and yours. It's time to turn your gaze to the noble calling of husbands within the sacred covenant of marriage.

What do you see?

Let's get closer and watch for the very best God intended for sacred vows!

1. *Husbands are the leader and head of the household*: The Bible teaches that husbands are called to lead their families with wisdom, humility, and love, following the example of Christ's sacrificial leadership. Just as Christ is the head of the church, husbands are called to head their households, providing guidance, direction, and spiritual leadership.

2. *Husbands are providers and protectors*: Husbands have a responsibility to provide for the physical, emotional, and spiritual needs of their wives and families. This includes providing material support, guidance, protection, and emotional support. Husbands are called to care for and protect their wives and families, ensuring their well-being and security.
3. *Husbands have sacrificial love*: The Bible instructs husbands to love their wives as Christ loved the church, giving Himself up for her. This sacrificial love is characterized by selflessness, service, and a willingness to prioritize the needs and well-being of their wives over their own. Husbands are called to demonstrate Christ-like love in their actions, attitudes, and relationships within the marriage.

Roles of the Wife

The biblical role of the wife is a multifaceted tapestry woven with threads of love, respect, and service, reflecting the divine design for marital harmony and partnership. Rooted in timeless truths and guided by the example of virtuous women throughout history, the wife's role encompasses nurturing, support, companionship, and the strength and wisdom to stand alongside her husband through life's joys and challenges.

As you journey deeper into understanding this sacred calling, contemplate the beauty and depth of the wife's role in cultivating a Christ–centered marriage that glorifies God and blesses both partners. Through the lens of Scripture and the wisdom of generations past, wives can embrace their role with grace, dignity, and unwavering devotion, enriching the fabric of their marital bond and embodying the beauty of God's design for marriage.

Wives are God's love in action. Here's how they do it:

1. *Through respect and submission*: Wives are called to respect and submit to their husbands as to the Lord. This submission is not of inferiority but of mutual respect and honor within the marriage relationship. Wives are called to recognize and honor the leadership and authority of their husbands, trusting in their guidance and direction.
2. *With support as a helpmate*: Wives are called to be supportive partners to their husbands, assisting them in their roles as leaders and providers. This includes offering encouragement, counsel, and practical assistance in fulfilling the responsibilities of marriage and family life. Wives are called to stand by their husbands, supporting them in their endeavors and legacy.
3. *By a gentle spirit*: Wives are encouraged to cultivate inner beauty and character qualities such as gentleness, humility, and reverence. This gentle and respectful

demeanor is of great value in God's sight and contributes to the harmony and well-being of the marriage relationship. Even in challenging circumstances, wives are called to demonstrate respect, honor, and kindness towards their husbands.

Overall, the biblical roles of husbands and wives are intended to promote order, harmony, and mutual respect within the marital relationship. Both husbands and wives are called to fulfill their roles with love, humility, and a commitment to honoring God and serving one another in marriage.

The biblical roles of husbands and wives are not meant to encourage competition or dominance within marriage. Instead, they promote mutual love, respect, and partnership based on the principles of sacrificial love, mutual submission, and mutual respect.

In a biblical marriage designed by God, both spouses are called to serve and honor one another, recognizing each other's unique roles and contributions within the marriage relationship. Husband, you are called to lead your family with love and humility, sacrificially serving and caring for your wife as Christ loved the church. Wife, you are called to respect and submit to your husband, recognizing his leadership and authority within the household.

However, it's important to note that this submission is not one of inferiority or subjugation but of mutual respect and adoring honor within the marriage relationship. Both husband and wife are equal in value and dignity before God, and both are called to fulfill their roles with love, humility and a commitment to serving one another.

Ultimately, the biblical model of marriage is one of partnership, servanthood, cooperation, and mutual support, where both spouses work together in unity to fulfill God's purpose for their lives and marriage. This promotes harmony, peace, and flourishing within the marriage relationship rather than competition or dominance.

A deeper look into the difference between the non-biblical and biblical roles of husband and wife lies primarily in their foundation, principles, and outcomes within the marriage relationship.

In exploring the roles of husband and wife, it's vital to understand their significance through a biblical lens compared to non-biblical perspectives. Biblical roles are rooted in God's design for marriage, emphasizing mutual respect, sacrificial love, and unity in Christ. In contrast, non-biblical roles often prioritize self-interest, equality in a secular sense, or cultural norms over God's ordained principles. Understanding these distinctions guides us toward embracing God's intended purpose for marriage, fostering harmony, and honoring His divine plan.

Here are the differences between Non-Biblical Roles vs. Biblical Roles:

Non-Biblical Roles:

1. *Based on cultural norms*: Non-biblical roles of a husband and wife are often influenced by societal and cultural norms, which may vary significantly across different cultures and time periods. These roles may be shaped by secular ideologies, traditional gender roles, or personal preferences rather than biblical principles.
2. *Emphasis on equality and autonomy*: In non-biblical roles, there may be a greater emphasis on equality and individual autonomy within the marriage relationship. Husbands and wives may view themselves as equal partners with equal rights and responsibilities, and decisions may be made based on consensus or negotiation rather than hierarchical authority.
3. *Varied expectations*: Non-biblical roles of a husband and wife may encompass a wide range of expectations and behaviors, depending on cultural, social, and personal factors. These roles may be flexible and adaptable to individual preferences, circumstances, and values.
4. *Potential for conflict and disunity*: Without a clear foundation in biblical principles, non-biblical roles of a husband and wife may lack a cohesive framework for resolving conflicts, making decisions, and prioritizing the well-being of the marriage relationship. This can lead to tensions, power struggles, and disunity within the marriage.

Biblical Roles:

1. *Rooted in Scripture*: The biblical roles of a husband and wife are grounded in the teachings and principles found in the Scriptures. They are based on God's design and purpose for marriage, as revealed in the Bible, providing a solid foundation for understanding the roles and responsibilities within the marriage relationship.
2. *Emphasis on servant leadership and mutual submission*: In biblical roles, a husband was called to lead their families with love and humility, sacrificially serving and caring for their wife as Christ loved the church. A wife is called to respect and submit to their husbands, recognizing their leadership and authority within the household. Both spouses are called to mutual submission, putting the needs and well-being of their spouse above their own.
3. *Clear expectations and guidelines*: The biblical roles of husbands and wives provide clear expectations and guidelines for behavior and conduct within the marriage relationship. They offer a framework for making decisions, resolving conflicts, and prioritizing the health and unity of the marriage.

4. *Promotion of harmony and unity:* Following biblical roles, husbands and wives can experience greater harmony, unity, and fulfillment within their marriage relationship. They are empowered to work together as partners, honoring God and serving one another with love, respect, and humility.

The difference between the non-biblical and biblical roles of husbands and wives lies in their foundation, principles, and outcomes within the marriage relationship. Biblical roles are rooted in Scripture, emphasize servant leadership and mutual submission, provide clear expectations and guidelines, and promote harmony and unity within the marriage.

THE IMPORTANCE OF COMMITMENT AND COVENANT

Commitment and Covenant in marriage are essential for cultivating a relationship that withstands the test of time and adversity. For clarity, commitment forms the bedrock of a strong marriage, providing stability, security, and trust between partners. Then, we have a covenant that underscores the lifelong nature of the commitment, emphasizing mutual care, sacrificial love, and the pursuit of unity and holiness together.

In a society where instant gratification and fleeting connections often overshadow the energy it takes for lasting commitments, understanding the depth and significance of commitment becomes paramount.

Commitment in marriage goes beyond mere dedication or obligation; it reflects a deep-seated resolve to honor the sacred bond between husband and wife. It signifies a willingness to prioritize the well-being of the marriage above individual desires or preferences, even when faced with challenges or hardships.

This commitment is not contingent upon feelings or circumstances but is rooted in steadfast devotion to the covenant made before God and witnesses.

Similarly, the concept of covenant underscores the sacred nature of marriage as a divine institution ordained by God. A covenant is more than a legal contract; it is a solemn promise, sealed with vows and upheld with integrity and faithfulness. Just as God is faithful to His covenant with His people, you are also called to uphold your covenant with one another, demonstrating unwavering loyalty and devotion through every season of life.

Commitment and Covenant in marriage advance an environment of trust, security, and stability within the relationship. It provides a solid foundation for building your lives together, knowing that you can rely on each other's unwavering support and fidelity. This sense of protection allows you to navigate challenges with confidence, knowing that you are united in your commitment to each other and to the marriage.

Furthermore, commitment and covenant serve as a powerful testimony to the world of God's faithfulness and grace. By honoring your vows and remaining steadfast in your commitment to each other, you bear witness to the transformative power of love and the redemptive work of God in your lives.

Your marriage becomes a living testament to the enduring nature of God's covenantal love, inspiring others to pursue relationships built on a foundation of commitment, fidelity, and unwavering devotion.

Commitment and covenant in marriage are essential for nurturing a relationship characterized by love, trust, and enduring devotion. By prioritizing your commitment to each other and honoring the sacred covenant of marriage, you create God's unfailing love and faithfulness.

Practical Exercises

Place a checkmark in the box what you are willing to commit to first.

- ♡ Set aside dedicated time to study key passages of Scripture that outline God's plan for marriage, such as Genesis 2:18-24 and Ephesians 5:21-33. Reflect on the principles and values inherent in these passages and discuss how they inform your understanding of marriage.

- ♡ Engage in a joint Bible study or devotional series focused on exploring God's plan for marriage. Use discussion questions and Reflection Questions to deepen your understanding and apply biblical principles to your relationship.

- ♡ Add a shared mission statement to the vision board for your marriage that incorporates the four pillars. Use this statement of purpose as a guiding framework for your relationship and decision-making processes.

What is your time frame for completing each exercise?

_____
_____
_____
_____
_____

What is the outcome you are looking for in each exercise?

_____
_____
_____
_____
_____

Reflection Questions

How does your current understanding of marriage align with God's plan outlined in Scripture?

What aspects of God's plan for marriage do you find most challenging or inspiring?

How can you deepen your commitment to living out God's plan for marriage in your relationship?

CHAPTER FOUR

COMMUNICATION IN MARRIAGE

"Do not let any unwholesome talk come out of your mouths, but only what is helpful for building others up according to their needs, that it may benefit those who listen."

~ Ephesians 4:29 (NIV)

Communication is essential for constructing trust, fostering understanding, and establishing a deep connection between spouses. Effective communication is not just about exchanging words; it's about loving well by listening actively, speaking kindly, and seeking to understand each other's hearts.

The key emphasis here lies in understanding the vital role of effective communication skills grounded in biblical principles. These skills are learned, not innate, underscoring the importance of intentionally cultivating them within the framework of marriage.

By nurturing these skills, you can increase deeper connection and understanding, aligning your communication with values of love, respect, and humility, as Scripture teaches. This intentional approach helps build a foundation for stronger relationships and a more fulfilling marital journey.

EFFECTIVE COMMUNICATION SKILLS BASED ON BIBLICAL PRINCIPLES

Effective communication in marriage is more than just exchanging words; it is about truly hearing and being heard, understanding and being understood, speaking truth in love, and navigating conflicts with grace and humility. It is a sacred dance of vulnerability and empathy, where you come together to share your hearts, dreams, and fears, forging a bond that transcends words.

There are secrets to uncover within effective communication in marriage and life when you engage in a culture of openness, respect, and mutual understanding, which enriches and deepens your togetherness.

"A truly wise person uses few words; a person with understanding is even-tempered. Even fools are thought wise when they keep silent; with their mouths shut, they seem intelligent" (Proverbs 17:27-28 NLT).

A truly wise person also listens to understand, as *St. Francis of Assisi's Prayer* shares with us; *"To be understood, as to understand."*[6] (**PRAYER OF ST. FRANSIS ASSISI** can be found in the Resources section towards the back of this book.)

Effective communication skills are a way to nurture understanding, connection, and unity within marriage. In all seasons of marital life, communication goes beyond the mere exchange of words; it encompasses listening, empathy, vulnerability, and mutual respect.

Active Listening

"A gentle answer turns away wrath, but a harsh word stirs up anger" (Proverbs 15:1 NIV).

Effective communication begins with active listening, attentively listening to each other's thoughts, feelings, and concerns without interruption or judgment, emphasizing the importance of humility, patience, and empathy in communication.

Here are key aspects of effective communication skills in marriage and the biblical principles for active listening:

Empathizing

Effective communication involves empathizing with your spouse's perspective and seeking to understand rather than being understood to validate their feelings and experiences. This reflects the biblical principle of bearing one another's burdens and showing empathy towards one another (Galatians 6:2, 1 Peter 3:8), demonstrating compassion and care in communication.

Respectful Expression

It requires clear and respectful expression of thoughts, feelings, and needs, avoiding criticism, defensiveness, or contempt. This aligns with the biblical principle of speaking the truth in love (Ephesians 4:15) and using words that build up rather than tear down (Ephesians 4:29), fostering an atmosphere of trust and safety in communication.

Resolving Conflicts

Effective communication involves resolving conflicts and disagreements constructively and respectfully, seeking reconciliation and understanding. This reflects the biblical principle of pursuing peace and reconciliation in relationships (Matthew 5:9, Matthew 18:15-17), prioritizing unity and harmony within the marriage.

Honoring Differences

Effective communication honors each spouse's godly differences and individuality, celebrating diversity and uniqueness within the marriage relationship. This aligns with the biblical principle of valuing diversity and honoring one another's gifts and strengths (1 Corinthians 12:12–27), recognizing that each spouse brings their purpose, perspective, and contributions to the marriage.

By incorporating these principles into your daily practice, you can cultivate a culture of openness, trust, and mutual respect within your marriage. You can navigate challenges, resolve conflicts, and deepen your connection with each other, strengthening your relationship and honoring God in your communication.

STRATEGIES FOR ACTIVE LISTENING AND EXPRESSING FEELINGS RESPECTFULLY

Now, it is time to lay the groundwork that forms the bedrock of effective communication in marriage. Active listening involves more than just hearing words—it requires a genuine effort to understand the emotions and intentions behind those words. It involves giving full attention, withholding judgment, and reflecting back on what you hear to ensure clarity and empathy.

On the other hand, expressing feelings respectfully involves articulating emotions honestly and sensitively, without blame or criticism. It is about communicating in a way that promotes understanding and constructive dialogue, even in moments of disagreement or conflict.

Together, the following strategies create a safe space where you both feel validated and valued, paving the way for deeper intimacy, mutual support, and a stronger marital bond, enhancing wedded bliss through harmony and strength.

Active listening allows you to wait for your turn to speak.

Start by giving your full attention: When your spouse is speaking, give them your undivided attention. Put away distractions such as phones or electronic devices and focus on what they say.

Be all in by using nonverbal cues: Show that you are engaged and attentive by making eye contact, nodding your head, and using affirmative gestures such as leaning forward or facing toward your spouse. These actions speak louder than your words to your loved one. It shows this relationship matters to you.

Prepare to paraphrase and reflect: After your spouse finishes speaking, paraphrase what they have said to ensure your understanding. Reflect back their feelings and concerns to demonstrate empathy and validation with your words. Wait for their acknowledgment that you heard correctly.

Courageously ask clarifying questions: If something is unclear or you need more information, ask open-ended questions to encourage your spouse to elaborate or clarify their thoughts and feelings.

Patiently avoid interrupting: Refrain from interrupting your spouse while they are speaking. Wait until they have finished before responding to ensure they feel heard and respected.

What you need to know about expressing feelings respectfully is that it starts with an "I."

Use "I" Statements: When expressing your feelings or concerns, use "I" statements to take ownership of your emotions and avoid placing blame. For example, say "I feel…" instead of "You always…"

Be specific: Clearly articulate your feelings and needs, using specific examples to illustrate your point. Avoid generalizations or sweeping statements that can lead to misunderstanding.

Focus on behavior, not character: When discussing issues or conflicts, focus on the specific behavior or action causing concern rather than attacking your spouse's character or personality. Stick to the topic, which is the primary concern being brought up for discussion.

Use a calm and gentle tone: Speak in a calm and gentle tone of voice, even when discussing difficult or sensitive topics. Avoid raising your voice or using harsh language that can escalate tensions.

Show empathy and understanding: Acknowledge and validate your spouse's feelings, even if you do not agree with them. Show empathy and understanding by listening attentively and responding with compassion.

Your thoughts shape your words, which are seeds that bear fruit. Align your thoughts with God's Word, and use words wisely, as they hold the power to uplift or to harm.

Adding these approaches to your communication habits can further an environment of attentive listening and thoughtful dialogue in your marriage, promoting empathy, understanding, and closeness with your spouse.

RESOLVING CONFLICTS IN A HEALTHY AND CHRIST-CENTERED MANNER

Conflicts are expected in any marriage, but how you manage them can either strengthen or weaken your relationship. Healthy boundaries in conflict resolution involve establishing guidelines for respectful dialogue and behavior during disagreements. This might include agreeing not to yell or name-call, taking breaks when emotions run high, and committing to resolving conflicts with mutual understanding rather than aiming to win an argument.

These boundaries create a safe space where you both can express yourselves without fear of judgment or hostility, fostering a spirit of cooperation and compromise.

Here are three key strategies for having healthy boundaries in effective communication:

1. *Take time-outs*: Agree to take breaks during arguments to cool down and reflect before continuing the discussion.
2. *No name-calling*: Establishing a boundary against using hurtful or demeaning language towards each other keeps communication flowing.
3. *Seek a resolution*: Committing to resolving conflicts with mutual understanding and compromise rather than focusing solely on winning the argument. Look for a win-win solution. If one wins an argument, both of you lose. Look for a win-win solution for reconciliation.

Conflicts in marriage arise from various sources, including differences in values, communication styles, priorities, and external stressors. However, conflicts themselves are not inherently negative; they present opportunities for growth, understanding, and deeper connection within the marriage relationship.

Resolving conflicts in a healthy and Christ-centered manner involves seven key principles:

1. Begin by seeking God's wisdom and guidance through prayer. Invite the Holy Spirit to lead you and your spouse in resolving the conflict with love, humility, and wisdom.

- *Prayer*: Start by praying sincerely, acknowledging your need for God's wisdom in your specific situation. Prayer opens up communication with God and invites His guidance into your life (James 1:5).
- *Scripture reading*: Dive into the Bible regularly to understand God's character, His will, and His principles. The Scriptures offer timeless wisdom and guidance for all areas of life (Psalm 119:105).
- *Quiet time*: Set aside dedicated time to listen to God through quiet reflection, a meditation on Scripture, and listening prayer. This allows space for God to speak to your heart and mind (Psalm 46:10).
- *Seeking counsel*: Seek wise counsel from mature believers, pastors, or Christian mentors who can offer biblically sound advice and perspective (Proverbs 15:22).
- Obeying God's Word: Actively obeying what God has already revealed in His Word prepares your heart to receive further guidance. Obedience demonstrates trust and readiness to follow God's leading (John 14:21).
- *Discernment*: Use discernment to distinguish between God's voice, your own desires, and external influences. The Holy Spirit provides discernment to guide you in making decisions aligned with God's will (1 John 4:1).
- *Patience and trust*: Trust that God's timing and ways are perfect, even when answers or directions may not come immediately. Patience allows God to work in His time and according to His purpose (Proverbs 3:5-6).

2. Take turns expressing your thoughts and feelings, practicing active listening and empathy towards each other. Seek to understand more about your spouse's perspective, validate their feelings, and refrain from interrupting or becoming defensive. Each agrees to listen attentively without interrupting when the other is speaking.
    - *Listen attentively*: Focus on what the other person is saying without thinking about your response.
    - *Wait for pauses*: Allow natural breaks in the conversation before speaking.
    - Use non-verbal cues: Nodding or making brief verbal affirmations ("I see," "Interesting") shows you're engaged without interrupting.
    - *Practice patience*: Be patient and avoid finishing someone's sentences or jumping in to express your thoughts.
    - *Ask questions*: Clarifying questions show interest and help you understand fully before responding.
    - *Respect boundaries*: Recognize when someone needs uninterrupted time to express themselves fully.

- *Reflect before responding*: Take a moment to process what was said before offering your input.

3. Speak Truth in Love. Express your thoughts, feelings, and needs honestly and respectfully to take ownership of your emotions. Speaking the truth in love means being mindful of your tone and demeanor and avoiding hurtful or inflammatory language. Speaking the truth in love is essential for effective communication and maintaining healthy relationships.
    - *Check your motives*: Ensure that your intention is genuinely to help or clarify rather than to criticize or control.
    - *Choose the right time and place*: Approach sensitive conversations when both of you are calm and receptive, and in a private setting if possible.
    - *Use "I" statements*: Express your feelings and observations from your perspective rather than making accusatory statements. For example, say, "I feel concerned when..." instead of "You always..."
    - *Be specific and clear*: Clearly articulate the issue or concern using concrete examples to avoid ambiguity.
    - *Listen actively*: Allow the other person to respond without interrupting, and genuinely listen to their perspective.
    - *Show empathy*: Acknowledge the other's feelings and viewpoints, even if you disagree.
    - *Avoid judgment and assumptions*: Stick to facts and avoid making assumptions about the other person's intentions or character.
    - *Focus on solutions*: Instead of dwelling on the problem, discuss possible solutions or compromises together. All solution ideas are welcomed in the discussion.
    - *Offer support*: Let the other know you are there to help and support them through any necessary changes.
    - *Seek mutual understanding*: Aim for a shared understanding and resolution that respects both your feelings and needs.

4. Seek Understanding and Compromise. Work together to find common ground and seek understanding, exploring potential solutions and compromises that address both your needs and concerns. Be willing to make concessions and find win-win solutions that honor both of you.
    - *Flexible solutions*: Be open to alternative approaches or methods that achieve the same goal but in different ways, accommodating different preferences.
    - *Shared responsibilities*: Divide tasks or responsibilities in a way that balances workload and acknowledges each person's strengths and abilities.

- *Creative problem-solving*: Finding new solutions that address underlying concerns or interests without compromising fundamental values or needs.
- *Future considerations*: Agree on a short-term solution with the understanding that it will be revisited or adjusted based on future developments or changes.
- *Incremental progress*: Taking small steps towards a larger goal or compromise, allowing for adjustments and improvements over time.
- *Acknowledgment of concerns*: Recognizing and addressing each other's concerns or fears through active listening and empathy can build trust and facilitate agreement.
- *Win-win mindset*: Focusing on mutual benefit and long-term relationship preservation rather than solely on immediate gains or losses.

5. Forgiveness and Reconciliation. Extend grace and forgiveness to each other, recognizing that we are all imperfect and need God's mercy. Let go of bitterness and resentment, choosing reconciliation and restoration of the relationship.
    - *Acknowledge and validate feelings*: Recognize and accept your emotions of bitterness and resentment without judgment. Understand that these feelings are normal reactions to hurt or injustice.
    - *Identify triggers and root causes*: Reflect on what triggers these emotions and try to identify the underlying reasons for your bitterness and resentment. Understanding the root causes can help you address them more effectively.
    - *Practice forgiveness*: Forgiveness is a deliberate decision to release feelings of resentment toward someone who has harmed you. It does not mean condoning their actions but rather freeing yourself from the negative emotions associated with the hurt.

        This process may involve
        - Acknowledging the pain caused.
        - Choosing to forgive is an act of the will.
        - Letting go of the desire for revenge or retribution.
        - Working towards empathy and understanding.
    - *Release negative thoughts*: Challenge negative thought patterns associated with bitterness and resentment. Replace them with positive affirmations or thoughts that promote healing and peace.
    - *Cultivate empathy and compassion*: Try to understand the perspective of the person who hurt you or caused resentment. Empathy can help soften feelings of bitterness and facilitate forgiveness.

- *Practice self-compassion*: Be kind to yourself throughout this process. Recognize that healing takes time and effort, and it's okay to seek support from trusted friends, family, or a counselor.
- *Focus on the present and future*: Instead of dwelling on past grievances, focus on the present moment and future goals. Engage in activities that bring you joy and fulfillment.
- *Seek spiritual guidance:* For those with a spiritual or religious belief system, seeking guidance and support through prayer, meditation, or seeking counsel from a spiritual leader can be beneficial in the process of forgiveness and letting go.

6. Seek Wise Counsel. If necessary, seek wise counsel from a trusted pastor, mentor, or counselor who can provide biblical guidance and support in resolving the conflict. Be open to receiving feedback and insights to help you navigate the situation with wisdom and discernment.
    - *Develop a growth mindset*: Approach feedback as an opportunity for growth and learning rather than criticism. Embrace the belief that feedback can help you improve and develop personally and professionally.
    - *Be willing to listen*: Cultivate active listening skills by focusing on what is being said without immediately reacting or defending yourself. Pay attention to both verbal and non-verbal cues to fully understand the feedback.
    - *Stay calm and manage emotions*: Remain composed and manage any initial defensive or emotional reactions that may arise. Take deep breaths and maintain a neutral demeanor to stay open-minded.
    - *Seek clarification*: If the feedback is unclear or ambiguous, ask clarifying questions to ensure you fully understand the perspective being shared. This demonstrates your commitment to understanding and learning.
    - *Reflect and evaluate*: Take time to reflect on the feedback provided. Consider how it aligns with your goals, values, and areas for improvement. Evaluate the validity and relevance of the feedback to gain insights into your behavior or performance.
    - *Express gratitude*: Regardless of whether the feedback is positive or constructive, express gratitude for the insights shared. This shows respect for the person providing feedback and encourages ongoing open communication.
    - *Act on feedback*: Use the feedback received as a catalyst for action. Develop an action plan or set specific goals to address areas for improvement or capitalize on strengths identified through feedback.

- *Seek support if needed*: If receiving feedback triggers strong emotions or challenges, seek support from a mentor, coach, or trusted colleague. Discussing your reactions and exploring strategies for growth can provide valuable perspective.

7. Be Committed to Growth and Change. Use conflicts as opportunities for personal and relational growth, commit to learning from the experience, and make positive changes in your attitudes, behaviors, and communication patterns. Cultivate humility, teachability, and a willingness to change for the better. Be the change you want to see in your marriage.
    - *Embrace a growth mindset*: Adopt the belief that your abilities and qualities can be developed through dedication and hard work. This mindset encourages learning from experiences, including mistakes and feedback.
    - *Seek feedback*: Actively seek constructive feedback from others, whether it's from mentors, colleagues, or loved ones. Be open to hearing different perspectives and insights about your strengths and areas for improvement.
    - *Practice active listening*: Listen attentively and empathetically to others without interrupting or formulating responses in your mind. Show genuine interest in understanding their viewpoints and experiences.
    - *Reflect and self-assess*: Regularly reflect on your actions, decisions, and interactions with others. Assess how your behaviors align with your values and goals. Identify areas where you can grow and develop.
    - *Admit mistakes and learn from them*: Acknowledge when you make mistakes or fall short of expectations. Take responsibility for your actions and use these experiences as opportunities for learning and growth.
    - *Be open to change*: Embrace change as a natural part of life and personal development. Remain flexible and adaptable to new ideas, approaches, and ways of thinking that can lead to positive outcomes.
    - *Practice humility*: Recognize your strengths and accomplishments without arrogance or pride. Value the contributions of others and appreciate their perspectives, skills, and experiences.
    - *Set goals for personal growth*: Establish specific, achievable goals that challenge you to improve and develop. Regularly assess your progress and celebrate milestones along the way.
    - *Seek accountability*: Engage with trusted individuals who can hold you accountable for your commitments and aspirations. Share your goals and progress with them and welcome their encouragement and support.

- *Stay curious and continuously learn*: Cultivate a curiosity for new knowledge, skills, and experiences. Invest time in lifelong learning through reading, courses, workshops, and meaningful conversations.

The Serenity Prayer[7] shows the difference between changing what you can (only yourself) or another (which you cannot). (The **SERENITY PRAYER** can be found in the Resources section at the back of this book.)

Only God can change a person's heart.

I know this to be true because that is how we became a Christ–centered couple. I sought to change my husband from the beginning, but it was only when he felt God's influence on his heart that he truly changed. I changed when I felt convicted by the Holy Spirit and went to God seeking forgiveness. I became the change I wanted to see in my marriage and life.

By approaching conflicts in marriage with a Christ–centered mindset, you can transform challenges or obstacles into opportunities for deeper intimacy, growth, and spiritual maturity. Through prayer, active listening, empathy, forgiveness, and a commitment to reconciliation, conflicts can become stepping stones toward a stronger, more resilient, and more Christ–centered marriage.

In the realm of marriage, effective communication is not just about the words spoken but also about the boundaries that shape how those words are received and understood. Healthy boundaries in communication ensure that each spouse feels heard and respected. For example, setting boundaries around interrupting each other or speaking respectfully, even in times of disagreement, can prevent misunderstandings and emotional hurt. When both of you agree to respect these boundaries, communication becomes a tool for building unity rather than division. Healthy boundaries keep you emotionally safe.

Practical Exercises

Check the box next to the task you intend to complete.

- ♡ *Mirror Exercise*: Take turns speaking about a topic while the listener mirrors back what they heard without adding interpretation or judgment. This exercise promotes active listening and ensures both partners understand each other accurately.

- ♡ Conflict Resolution Role-Play: Role-play a recent or hypothetical conflict using assertive communication techniques. Practice expressing feelings using "I" statements and actively listening without interruption. Afterward, discuss what worked well and what could be improved.

- ♡ *Daily Check-In*: Set aside time each day to share three things: one thing you appreciate about your spouse, one challenge you faced together or individually, and one goal or hope for the future. This exercise nurtures ongoing connection and emotional support.

What did the Holy Spirit reveal to you as you did this exercise?

_____

_____

_____

_____

What are the most important things to discuss?

_____

_____

_____

_____

Reflection Questions

What communication patterns from your family of origin influence how you communicate in your marriage? How can you adapt or change these patterns to improve communication with your spouse?

_____

_____

_____

_____

_____

In what ways do you currently feel understood and valued by your spouse in your communication? What steps can you take to enhance this sense of understanding and value?

_____

_____

_____

_____

_____

Think about a recent conflict. How did communication (or lack thereof) contribute to the outcome? What could you both do differently next time to navigate conflict more effectively and peacefully?

_____

_____

_____

_____

_____

Through these practical exercises and reflection questions, you can deepen your understanding of the biblical foundations of marriage and strengthen your relationship accordingly.

CHAPTER FIVE

NURTURING INTIMACY

"You are altogether beautiful, my love; there is no flaw in you."

~ Song of Solomon 4:7 (ESV)

What do you see when you look in a mirror? What are the words you hear?

If you're like most people, you hear the negative louder than you hear the positive. Yet, God reminds us that He sees each one of us as flawless because He made us in His own image. He sees each of us as perfect.

Intimacy is the heartbeat of marriage, the sacred space where two souls intertwine, hearts beat as one, and love flourishes in its purest form. In this chapter, we delve into the art of nurturing intimacy within marriage, exploring the myriad ways in which you can deepen your connection, cultivate closeness, and experience the fullness of marital love.

Nurturing intimacy is your first stop on a personal journey that goes beyond mere physical closeness. It involves cultivating emotional connection, spiritual unity, and deep mutual understanding. Intimacy thrives on trust, vulnerability, and the willingness to be fully known and accepted by your spouse. It encompasses not just moments of passion and romance but also the everyday gestures of kindness, empathy, and support that strengthen the bond between partners. When you begin to discover that intimacy is nurtured through intentional communication, shared experiences, and commitment, you will want to prioritize each other's needs and well-being. It's about creating a safe and sacred space to freely express your deepest thoughts, desires, and fears, knowing you are cherished and valued. Through nurturing intimacy, you can experience a richness and depth in your relationship that enhances your emotional connection and brings joy and fulfillment to your life together.

It encompasses an emotional, physical, and spiritual connection that plays a crucial role in nurturing intimacy by safeguarding each one's emotional and physical well-being.

> *Intimacy is the heartbeat of marriage, the sacred space where two souls intertwine, hearts beat as one, and love flourishes in its purest form.*

To give you an idea of what this looks like, consider:

Respecting each other's need for personal space and physical boundaries, such as privacy in personal hygiene routines or time alone.

We must be mindful of each other's emotional needs and sensitive to sharing personal thoughts and feelings at appropriate times.

Agreeing on boundaries around physical intimacy, including mutual consent, respect for each other's desires and comfort levels, and openness to discuss preferences and concerns.

Intimacy also enriches and sustains the marriage bond. From heartfelt conversations and shared dreams to tender gestures and acts of service, intimacy flourishes in the daily rhythms of life, weaving a tapestry of love, trust, and commitment that stands the test of time.

Embrace the sacred privilege of intimacy, cherishing the gift of marriage and the boundless depths of love that it holds.

PHYSICAL, EMOTIONAL, AND SPIRITUAL INTIMACY IN MARRIAGE

Physical, emotional, and spiritual intimacy forms the cornerstone of a thriving and fulfilling marriage, weaving together the intricate threads of connection, trust, and love between spouses. In exploring these dimensions of intimacy, you will begin to uncover the depth and richness of a marital union, as well as the transformative power it holds within the sacred covenant of marriage.

Physical intimacy encompasses the tangible expressions of love and affection shared between husband and wife. It involves not only sexual intimacy but also the simple yet profound acts of touch, embrace, and physical closeness that communicate care, desire, and devotion. Song of Solomon 4:7 beautifully portrays physical intimacy within marriage, where the husband and wife delight in each other's bodies and celebrate the gift of sexual union as a reflection of God's love for His people. Marriage is the bigger picture of a loving God in an intimate sacred covenant.

Emotional intimacy touches the realm where the spirit, mind, will, and emotions meet. Sharing your deepest thoughts, feelings, and vulnerabilities with one another is possible. It involves open communication, empathetic listening, and mutual support, creating a safe and nurturing environment where you both feel seen, heard, and valued. Emotional intimacy nurtures trust, empathy, and understanding within the marital relationship, strengthening your bond and deepening your connection on a soulful level.

Spiritual intimacy transcends the physical and emotional realms, drawing you into a deeper relationship with God and each other. It involves shared faith, prayer, worship, and spiritual growth as you journey together in your walk with Christ and support one another in your spiritual journeys.

Spiritual intimacy enriches the marital relationship, providing a foundation of shared values, beliefs, and purpose that guides and sustains you through the joys and challenges of life. Together, physical, emotional, and spiritual intimacy form a holistic and interconnected tapestry of marital union, weaving together the various dimensions of human experience and drawing you into a deeper and more profound relationship with one another. As you nurture intimacy, the fullness of God's design for marital unity, finding strength, joy, and fulfillment becomes your shared journey of love and companionship.

To truly love well through healthy boundaries in marriage involves understanding and respecting each other's needs, emotions, and personal space while maintaining a strong and united relationship.

How can it work for you as a couple?

By establishing healthy boundaries, you show respect for each other's individuality and personal space. It allows your spouse, as well as yourself, to feel valued and honored in the relationship, fostering a sense of mutual respect and dignity.

Setting healthy boundaries helps protect emotional well-being by preventing issues like resentment, codependency, and emotional burnout. It encourages open communication about feelings and needs without fear of judgment or neglect.

Healthy boundaries allow each spouse to maintain their personal identity and pursue individual interests and goals outside of the marriage. This promotes personal growth and fulfillment, which ultimately strengthens the marital bond.

Boundaries facilitate healthier conflict resolution by providing clear guidelines for communication and behavior. By addressing disagreements without crossing each other's emotional or physical limits, you can lead to more constructive and respectful interactions.

Respecting boundaries builds trust within the marriage. When each spouse feels their boundaries are honored, they are more likely to trust their spouse and feel secure in the relationship.

Overall, loving well through healthy boundaries in marriage involves intentional communication, mutual understanding, and a commitment to honoring each other's needs and preferences. It creates a supportive environment where both spouses can thrive individually and together, contributing to a strong and fulfilling marital relationship.

CULTIVATING INTIMACY THROUGH QUALITY TIME AND SHARED EXPERIENCES

Cultivating intimacy through quality time and shared experiences lies at the heart of a biblical marriage designed by God—Himself. In the sacred covenant of marriage, God calls husbands and wives to prioritize their relationship, investing time and effort into nurturing intimacy and connection on a daily basis. As you engage in meaningful activities together and intentionally carve out moments for quality time, they deepen their bond and strengthen the foundation of their marriage in alignment with God's design.

Quality time in marriage involves more than mere presence; it entails intentional engagement, active listening, and genuine interaction between spouses. It is about setting aside distractions and making space for each other in the midst of busy schedules and responsibilities, demonstrating love, respect, and prioritization of the marital relationship. In Mark 6:31-32, *"Then, because so many people were coming and going that they did not even have a chance to eat, he said to them, "Come with me by yourselves to a quiet place and get some rest." So they went away by themselves in a boat to a solitary place"* (NIV).

We see Jesus modeling the importance of quality time and shared experiences in His relationship with His disciples. He often withdrew with them to solitary places to rest and spend time together.

Shared experiences further enhance intimacy within marriage as you create lasting memories and deepen your connection through shared activities, adventures, and milestones. Whether exploring new places, pursuing shared interests, or simply enjoying each other's company in everyday moments, shared experiences foster unity, joy, and companionship within the marital relationship.

In Ecclesiastes 4:9-12, we are reminded of the strength and support found in companionship, *"A person standing alone can be attacked and defeated, but two can stand back-to-back and conquer. Three are even better, for a triple-braided cord is not easily broken"* (NLT).

As you cultivate intimacy through quality time and shared experiences, you honor God's design for marriage and bear witness to His love and faithfulness in your relationship. You create a sanctuary of love and unity within your home, where God's presence dwells and His blessings abound. By prioritizing your relationship, investing in each other's lives, and sharing life's joys and challenges together, you embody the beauty and significance of a biblical marriage.

OVERCOMING OBSTACLES TO INTIMACY

Overcoming obstacles to intimacy is vital to nurturing a healthy and thriving marriage following God's design. While intimacy is a cornerstone of marital unity, it is not immune to challenges and barriers hindering its growth and development. In navigating these obstacles, you are called to lean on each other, trust in God's guidance, and actively work together to overcome the barriers that threaten to undermine your intimacy.

One common obstacle to intimacy is communication breakdowns.

Poor communication can lead to misunderstandings, conflict, and emotional distance between spouses.

Examples of this would be:

- *Communication issues*: Misunderstandings often stem from poor communication, where messages are misinterpreted or not effectively conveyed. This can lead to frustration, confusion, and a sense of disconnect.
- *Unmet expectations*: When you have differing expectations about roles, responsibilities, or emotional support within the marriage, it can create conflict. Unrealistic or uncommunicated expectations can lead to feelings of disappointment and resentment.
- *Conflict avoidance*: Avoiding conflict altogether can result in emotional distance. Unresolved issues simmer beneath the surface, leading to a lack of intimacy and openness in the relationship.
- *Lack of emotional connection*: Emotional distance may occur when you feel unsupported or neglected emotionally. This can happen due to busy schedules, differing priorities, or unresolved past hurts.
- *Stress and external pressures*: External stressors such as financial difficulties, job pressures, or health issues can strain a marriage, causing emotional distance as you focus on managing external challenges rather than nurturing your relationship.
- *Different communication styles*: You may have contrasting ways of expressing and interpreting emotions, which can lead to misunderstandings and conflicts if not understood or accommodated.
- *Lack of intimacy*: Physical and emotional intimacy are essential for maintaining closeness in a marriage. Emotional distance can grow when intimacy wanes or is neglected, affecting the overall connection between spouses.

To overcome this barrier, you must prioritize open and honest communication, actively listen to each other's concerns, and seek to understand one another's perspectives with empathy and grace. By creating a culture of communication and vulnerability within your marriage, you can bridge the gap and cultivate deeper intimacy.

Another obstacle to intimacy is unresolved conflict and past hurts.

When unresolved issues linger beneath the surface, you can create walls of resentment and bitterness that impede emotional connection and trust between spouses. To overcome this barrier, you must be willing to address and resolve conflicts in a healthy and constructive manner, seeking forgiveness, reconciliation, and healing. By extending grace and forgiveness to one another, you can break down the barriers that hinder intimacy and experience restoration in your relationship.

External stressors such as work pressures, financial difficulties, and family responsibilities can also obstruct intimacy within marriage. When you are overwhelmed by external demands, you may struggle to prioritize your relationship and invest time and energy into nurturing intimacy.

To overcome this barrier, setting healthy boundaries will help to manage stress effectively and intentionally carve out moments for quality time and connection. By prioritizing your relationship and supporting each other through life's challenges, you can strengthen your bond and overcome obstacles to intimacy.

Ultimately, overcoming obstacles and turning them into opportunities for intimacy requires a commitment to growth, resilience, and faith in God's provision and guidance. By leaning on each other for support, seeking God's wisdom and strength, and actively working together to address challenges, you can navigate the ups and downs of married life with grace and perseverance.

Here are some ways to help you to lean on each other:

- *Open communication*: Expressing your needs, concerns, and emotions openly and honestly allows your partner to understand how they can support you effectively.
- *Active listening*: Being attentive and empathetic when your partner shares their feelings or struggles helps build a supportive atmosphere where both feel heard and valued.
- *Offering encouragement*: Providing words of encouragement and affirmation during challenging times can uplift your partner's spirits and strengthen their resolve.
- *Practical assistance*: Offering practical help, such as sharing household responsibilities and childcare duties or assisting with tasks, shows your commitment to easing your partner's burden.

- *Emotional support*: Providing emotional reassurance, understanding, and validation during difficult situations or decisions can be crucial for maintaining trust and intimacy.
- *Being present*: Making time to be physically and emotionally present for each other, especially during times of stress or crisis, reinforces your commitment to mutual support.
- *Seeking help together*: When challenges seem overwhelming, seeking guidance from a trusted counselor, pastor, or mentor as a couple can provide additional support and perspective.

Through prayer, communication, and mutual support, you can overcome obstacles to intimacy and cultivate a marriage that honors God and reflects His love and grace.

In nurturing intimacy, couples often face obstacles such as communication barriers, unresolved conflicts, emotional distance, and differences in emotional needs. Overcoming these challenges requires openness, vulnerability, and a commitment to understanding each other's perspectives. Building trust, practicing active listening, and addressing past hurts are crucial steps toward fostering deeper emotional connection and intimacy in a relationship.

In addition to communication barriers, unresolved conflicts, emotional distance, and differences in emotional needs, nurturing intimacy also involves addressing issues of trust and vulnerability. Trust can be undermined by past betrayals or misunderstandings, requiring deliberate efforts to rebuild through transparency and consistency.

Addressing trust and vulnerability issues in a relationship involves navigating deep emotional terrain with sensitivity and care. Trust can be fragile, often shaped by past experiences of betrayal, disappointment, or neglect.

Rebuilding trust requires consistent honesty, reliability, and transparency from both partners. It's about showing through actions and words that you can be relied upon and that your intentions are genuine. Vulnerability, however, entails opening up emotionally and allowing yourself to be seen and understood by your spouse.

This requires courage and a willingness to share fears, insecurities, and innermost thoughts without fear of judgment or rejection. Building a safe environment where vulnerability is welcomed involves creating a nonjudgmental space where partners feel secure enough to express themselves authentically. Overcoming trust issues and fostering vulnerability cultivates a deeper connection and intimacy, as it strengthens the emotional bond between partners.

Emotional wounds from previous experiences or childhood can significantly affect how you connect emotionally within your relationship, impacting your marriage. These wounds often necessitate empathy and patience in understanding each other's triggers and sensitivities, as they frequently stem from past traumas, such as:

- *Childhood abuse or neglect*: Physical, emotional, or sexual abuse during childhood can profoundly impact trust and emotional security in adult relationships.
- *Family dysfunction*: Growing up in a household with addiction, mental illness, or constant conflict can create lasting emotional wounds and difficulty forming healthy relationships.
- *Loss or grief*: The death of a loved one, especially in childhood or adolescence, can lead to unresolved grief that affects future relationships.
- *Divorce or family separation*: Witnessing or experiencing parental divorce or separation can shape beliefs about commitment and stability in relationships.
- *Bullying or peer rejection*: Childhood experiences of bullying, social rejection, or exclusion can influence self-esteem and trust in others.
- *Accidents or serious illness:* Personal experiences of trauma such as accidents, serious illness, or medical procedures can lead to fear, anxiety, and a need for control in relationships.
- *Cultural or religious trauma*: Experiences of discrimination, persecution, or religious indoctrination can impact identity and interpersonal trust.

Neglect from past experiences or childhood trauma can manifest in various ways, impacting individuals in their adult lives:

- *Emotional neglect*: This involves caregivers failing to meet emotional needs, such as providing affection, validation, or emotional support. Adults who experience emotional neglect may struggle with intimacy, have difficulty expressing emotions, or feel unworthy of love.
- *Physical neglect*: Physical neglect refers to caregivers failing to provide basic physical needs, such as food, shelter, clothing, or medical care. Adults who experience physical neglect may have challenges with self-care, struggle with feelings of insecurity, or have difficulty trusting others.
- *Educational neglect*: When caregivers fail to provide adequate educational opportunities or support, it can lead to difficulties in academic achievement, self-confidence issues, or challenges in pursuing career goals.
- *Supervisory neglect*: This occurs when caregivers fail to adequately supervise and protect children, exposing them to unsafe situations or environments. Adults who experience supervisory neglect may have issues with boundary-setting, struggle with trust in relationships, or exhibit hypervigilance.

- *Neglect of socialization*: Lack of opportunities for social interaction and development can result in difficulties in forming and maintaining relationships in adulthood. Adults who experience social neglect may feel isolated, have limited social skills, or struggle with feelings of loneliness.

Abandonment can take various forms, and its effects can deeply impact individuals:

- *Physical abandonment*: This occurs when a caregiver or significant person in a child's life physically leaves or is absent for extended periods without adequate support or care. This can lead to feelings of insecurity, fear of abandonment in relationships, or difficulty trusting others.
- *Emotional abandonment*: Emotional abandonment happens when caregivers are emotionally unavailable, neglecting the child's emotional needs, such as affection, validation, or empathy. Adults who experience emotional abandonment may struggle with intimacy, have challenges expressing emotions, or feel unworthy of love.
- *Psychological abandonment*: Psychological abandonment involves caregivers who are present physically but emotionally distant or neglectful. This can lead to feelings of loneliness, emotional numbness, or a sense of not being understood.
- *Financial abandonment*: Financial abandonment occurs when caregivers fail to provide financial support or stability, leaving the child without basic necessities or opportunities. Adults who experience financial abandonment may struggle with financial management, have difficulty establishing stability, or feel insecure about their future.
- *Abandonment trauma*: Chronic or severe abandonment experiences can result in abandonment trauma, where individuals develop deep-seated fears, insecurities, or patterns of behavior that stem from these early experiences. This can impact self-esteem, relationships, and overall well-being.

Dysfunctional family dynamics can manifest in various ways, often characterized by unhealthy patterns of behavior, communication, and relationships among family members. Here are some common signs of dysfunctional family dynamics:

- *Poor communication*: Communication is often ineffective, marked by misunderstandings, conflicts, or avoidance of difficult topics. Family members may struggle to express their feelings openly or listen empathetically to each other.

- *Lack of boundaries*: Boundaries, both physical and emotional, may be poorly defined or disregarded. This can lead to intrusion into personal space, over-involvement in each other's lives, or difficulty respecting individual privacy.
- *Unresolved conflict*: Conflict within the family is frequent and often unresolved. Issues may be swept under the rug or ignored, leading to simmering resentment, passive-aggressive behavior, or explosive arguments.
- *Role confusion*: Roles and responsibilities within the family may be unclear or rigidly enforced. This can result in role reversals where children may take on adult responsibilities prematurely, or parents may fail to fulfill their parental roles effectively.
- *Emotional instability*: Emotional expression within the family is erratic or suppressed. Family members may experience mood swings, emotional outbursts, or emotional numbness as a result of unaddressed feelings or past traumas.
- *Substance abuse or addiction*: Dysfunctional families may struggle with substance abuse issues or addictive behaviors, which can exacerbate existing conflicts and impair family functioning.
- *Control issues*: Control dynamics may be prevalent, with one or more family members exerting undue influence or manipulation over others. This can lead to feelings of powerlessness, resentment, or rebellion among family members.
- *Lack of support*: Emotional support and validation may be lacking or inconsistent within the family. Family members may feel isolated, unsupported, or disconnected from each other's needs and emotions.

These can shape one's beliefs about trust, love, and intimacy. Traumas and dysfunctions within families can vary widely but often include issues such as neglect, abandonment, emotional or physical abuse, substance abuse, poor communication, role confusion, and lack of boundaries.

These factors can lead to emotional instability, unresolved conflict, control issues, and a lack of support within the family unit. Addressing these challenges typically involves therapy or counseling to improve communication, establish healthy boundaries, heal past wounds, and foster supportive and functional relationships among family members.

In nurturing intimacy, these wounds may manifest as fear of vulnerability, difficulty in expressing emotions, or an inclination towards self-protection. Due to these unresolved emotional scars, you may struggle to fully open up or trust your spouse. Addressing these wounds involves recognizing their influence on your current relationship dynamics and working together to create a safe space for healing. It may involve therapy, open communication, and mutual support to gradually build trust and encourage emotional expression without fear of retribution or abandonment. By acknowledging and addressing these emotional wounds, couples can foster deeper emotional connection and intimacy based on mutual understanding and healing.

Creating a safe and sacred space for open communication involves setting aside time for meaningful conversations, actively listening without judgment, and validating each other's feelings. Ultimately, overcoming these obstacles nurtures a deeper emotional bond and strengthens the foundation of intimacy in marriage.

Nurturing intimacy in marriage is a deep connection that goes far beyond physical closeness. It involves emotional vulnerability, mutual trust, and an intense understanding of each other's innermost thoughts, desires, and fears. When you can authentically share these aspects of yourself with another, it creates a bond that is not only fulfilling but also spiritually enriching.

This level of intimacy raises a sense of oneness and unity, where both feel truly seen, heard, and valued by the other. It's a sacred space where unconditional love, empathy, and acceptance flourish, reflecting a glimpse of the deep connection and harmony described in spiritual beliefs.

Practical Exercises

Place a checkmark in the box next to the task you plan to accomplish.

- ♡ Schedule regular date nights with your spouse to prioritize quality time together. Set aside a specific evening each week or bi-weekly where you can focus solely on each other without distractions.

- ♡ Learn each other's Love Language.[8]

- ♡ Plan activities that you both enjoy, such as going for a walk, trying a new restaurant, or watching a movie at home. Use this time to reconnect, communicate openly, and deepen your emotional and physical intimacy.

What steps will you take to ensure you complete these practical exercises together as a couple?

_____

_____

_____

_____

_____

How can you hold each other accountable for following through on these exercises and integrating them into your daily lives?

_____

_____

_____

_____

_____

In what ways do you anticipate these exercises strengthening your commitment to each other and enhancing your relationship moving forward?

Reflection Questions

How do you currently prioritize quality time and intimacy in your marriage, and what changes can you make to enhance this aspect of your relationship?

Reflect on past experiences where you and your spouse felt most connected and intimate. What factors contributed to these moments, and how can you recreate them in your daily lives?

In what ways do you communicate your love and affection for your spouse? How can you express intimacy beyond physical affection, such as through acts of service, words of affirmation, or shared experiences?

CHAPTER SIX

BUILDING A STRONG FOUNDATION

"Can two walk together, unless they are agreed?"

~ Amos 3:3 (NKJV)

Building a Christ-centered marriage that lasts requires fundamentals, such as being grounded in shared values. Amos 3:3 is a reminder that to walk in unity; there must be agreement and alignment in your relationship with God and each other.

This concept not only helps you weather the storms and navigate challenges but also aligns your hearts with God and each other, creating a sturdy framework to build a resilient and thriving marital relationship and experience the fullness of God's blessings within your marital union.

Just as a solid covering on a structure withstands the elements underneath, a marriage built on trust, communication, and mutual respect can endure and thrive through every season of life as a covering for marriage. It is by honoring God and reflecting His love and grace that I am blessed to share with you.

Creating a plan with common goals and core values (**CORE VALUES FOR YOU AND YOUR FUTURE TOGETHER** which can be found in the Resource section at the back of the book), sharing big dreams, and discovering the purpose of your marriage is a fundamental step in building a strong foundation for marriage.

The importance of unity and alignment in marriage: As you come together to discern and pursue shared goals, dreams, and values, you establish common ground, receive a framework for decision-making, conflict resolution, and mutual support, and strengthen the bond of unity within your marriage.

A Christ-centered marriage requires intentional cultivation and nurturing of faith through prayer and spiritual growth. In James 5:16, James talks about the power of prayer in the life of believers: *"The prayer of a righteous person is powerful and effective"* (NIV). By prioritizing prayer and seeking God's guidance and wisdom in all aspects of your marriage, you invite His presence and provision into your relationship, deepening your faith and trust in Him as the foundation of your marriage.

As you explore the themes of establishing common goals and values and nurturing faith through prayer, be inspired to build a strong foundation for your marriage that honors God and reflects His love and grace. Together, embrace the journey of building a

Christ–centered marriage that stands firm against the storms of life, rooted in unity, faith, and the transformative power of God's love.

ESTABLISHING COMMON GOALS AND VALUES AS A COUPLE

Establishing common goals and values for you as a couple is paramount in building a strong and thriving marriage. It provides a shared vision and direction, nurturing unity, mutual understanding, and cooperation.

Here's how:

Establishing a shared vision and direction in marriage provides a unifying framework that promotes unity, mutual understanding, and cooperation. When both of you align on your goals and aspirations for the future, it creates a sense of purpose and direction. This shared vision serves as a compass or plumbline, guiding decisions and actions toward common objectives.

> *Establishing a shared vision and direction in marriage provides a unifying framework that promotes unity, mutual understanding, and cooperation.*

When partners share a common understanding of their future together, they are more likely to openly discuss their thoughts, feelings, and concerns, which fosters effective communication. This mutual understanding reduces misunderstandings and promotes empathy while respecting the other's perspective within the context of your shared vision.

Conflict resolution also benefits from a shared vision as it provides a reference point for finding solutions that align with your long-term goals. During conflicts, you can draw on your shared vision to prioritize the relationship over individual differences, seeking compromises that honor each other's aspirations.

Similarly, decision-making becomes more collaborative and less contentious when guided by a shared vision. Together, you can weigh options against your shared goals, ensuring that choices support your collective future rather than solely satisfying immediate desires.

Seeking the Lord's guidance has been pivotal in my marriage journey. By prioritizing His plan and seeking His wisdom, my spouse and I have navigated challenges with clarity and unity. It has helped us make decisions that strengthen our bond and honor our commitment to each other and to God's purpose for our marriage.

I used the same concept when launching my counseling ministry. I sought the Lord's guidance as the cornerstone of my endeavor. I sought His plan for the counseling center, discerning which opportunities aligned with His will and knowing when to decline others gracefully.

In essence, a shared vision and direction in marriage and other aspects of life nurture unity, mutual understanding, and cooperation by providing a solid foundation for effective communication, conflict resolution, and decision-making. This alignment helps you to navigate challenges together, strengthening your bond and fostering a resilient marital relationship.

Moreover, it lays the foundation for effective communication, conflict resolution, and decision-making within the marital relationship.

Another one of the key reasons why it is important to establish common goals and values is that it creates alignment and harmony in your marriage. When spouses are on the same page regarding their aspirations, priorities, and values, you can work together as a team to pursue your shared vision and overcome obstacles that may arise along the way.

This alignment promotes a sense of unity and partnership, strengthening the bond between you and promoting a deep sense of connection and belonging within the marriage.

Establishing common goals and values also provides clarity and direction. It helps you to identify what is most important to you as individuals and as a couple, allowing you to prioritize your time, energy, and resources accordingly.

Common goals and values in a marriage can encompass a wide range of areas that are meaningful and significant to both of you.

Here are some examples:

- *Spiritual growth*: Both spouses prioritize their faith and seek to deepen their spiritual connection individually and as a couple. This may include attending religious services, praying, or participating in spiritual retreats.
- *Family planning*: Shared goals around family planning can include decisions about the number of children, parenting styles, and the values and principles you may wish to instill in your children.
- *Career and financial goals*: You may have shared aspirations regarding career advancement, financial stability, savings goals, investments, and long-term financial planning.
- *Personal development*: By prioritizing personal growth and development, whether through continuing education, pursuing hobbies and interests, or working on personal wellness and health goals.

- *Community and social engagement*: Shared values in this area might involve volunteering together, supporting charitable causes, or being actively involved in community events and organizations.
- *Relationship dynamics*: Goals related to the marriage itself, such as improving communication, strengthening emotional connection, nurturing intimacy, and maintaining a healthy work-life balance.
- *Travel and leisure*: Shared interests in travel destinations, cultural experiences, and recreational activities that both enjoy and look forward to experiencing together.
- *Environmental and lifestyle choices*: Values that are related to sustainability, eco-conscious living, healthy lifestyle choices (such as diet and exercise), and maintaining a balanced approach to life's demands.

These goals and values serve as guiding principles that shape the marriage's decisions, actions, and priorities. When you both align on these fundamental aspects, it enhances unity, mutual support, and cooperation, fostering a strong foundation in your relationship.

By setting clear goals and defining shared values, you can create a blueprint for your future together, making intentional choices that align with your vision for your marriage and family life.

Here are some ideas to help you:

To align with your shared vision for a Christ-centered marriage, here are some initial choices each spouse can consider making.

- Start each day with prayer individually and together, seeking God's guidance and wisdom for your marriage and family.
- Make a commitment to open, honest, and respectful communication. Practice active listening and strive to understand each other's perspectives.
- Establish healthy boundaries that honor each other's needs and cultivate mutual respect. This includes boundaries around time, personal space, and emotional availability.
- Encourage and support each other's spiritual growth by attending church together, participating in Bible studies, and engaging in spiritual practices.
- Involve each other in decision-making processes, seeking consensus and unity in major life choices such as finances, parenting, and career decisions.
- Dedicate intentional time for nurturing your relationship, whether through date nights, shared hobbies, or quiet moments of connection.

- Commit to a culture of forgiveness and grace in your marriage. Address conflicts promptly, sincerely apologize when needed, and extend forgiveness generously.
- Be each other's cheerleader and source of encouragement. Celebrate each other's successes, provide emotional support during challenges, and affirm each other's strengths.

By aligning these initial choices with your shared vision for a Christ-centered marriage, you lay a strong foundation for the unity, mutual understanding, and cooperation in your relationship.

Additionally, establishing common goals and values promotes accountability and mutual support within the marriage. Promoting accountability and mutual support in a marriage involves several key practices:

- *Open communication*: Creating an environment where both of you feel safe to share your thoughts, feelings, and challenges without fear of judgment. This encourages transparency and honesty.
- *Setting goals together*: Establish mutual goals for your marriage, family, and personal growth. Regularly review and update these goals together to stay aligned and accountable to each other.
- *Check-ins and reviews*: Schedule regular check-ins to discuss progress toward your goals, address any concerns or setbacks, and celebrate achievements together. This promotes accountability and keeps both partners engaged in the shared journey.
- *Shared responsibilities*: Divide household chores, parenting duties, and other responsibilities fairly based on each other's strengths and preferences. Supporting each other in daily tasks fosters mutual respect and reduces feelings of overwhelm.
- Encouragement and affirmation: Build each other up through positive reinforcement and affirmation. Acknowledge efforts and achievements, no matter how small, to reinforce mutual support and strengthen emotional connection.
- *Accountability partnerships*: Consider seeking out a mentor couple or accountability partners within your faith community or marriage support network. These relationships can provide additional perspective, encouragement, and accountability.

- *Conflict resolution*: Handle conflicts constructively by listening actively, seeking understanding, and finding mutually agreeable solutions. This process promotes accountability by ensuring both spouses take responsibility for their actions and commitments.
- *Prayer and spiritual support*: Pray together regularly, seeking God's guidance and strength for your marriage. Spiritual practices such as studying Scripture together and attending church can also deepen mutual support and accountability.

By implementing these practices, you will create a supportive and accountable environment that strengthens your marriage and helps you to grow together in faith and love.

When you commit to pursuing your shared goals and upholding your shared values, you hold each other accountable for your actions and decisions, providing encouragement, motivation, and guidance along the way. This mutual accountability strengthens your bond and furthers a sense of teamwork as you work together to overcome challenges and achieve your shared aspirations.

The goals and values can vary depending on your unique circumstances and priorities as a couple. Some common goals (**CORE VALUES FOR YOU AND YOUR FUTURE TOGETHER** as referred to in the Resource Section at the back of the book) may include building a strong and healthy relationship, raising a family, pursuing career aspirations, and making a positive impact in your community. Similarly, shared values may include honesty, integrity, faithfulness, compassion, and service to others. By identifying your shared goals and values, you can cultivate a marriage that is grounded in mutual respect, understanding, and purpose, laying the foundation for a lifetime of love and happiness together.

STRENGTHENING MARRIAGE THROUGH PRAYER AND FAITH

A Christ–centered marriage necessitates strengthening through prayer and faith, aligning the marital relationship with God's divine plan and purpose. Prayer and faith serve as vital pillars that uphold the foundation of a Christ–centered marriage, fostering spiritual growth, unity, and resilience amidst life's challenges.

Prayer is the cornerstone of a Christ–centered marriage, as it invites God's presence, guidance, and blessing into the relationship. Through prayer, you cultivate a deeper intimacy with God and with each other as you lift up your joys, concerns, and needs before the Lord. Prayer allows you to surrender your worries and fears, trusting in God's providence and sovereignty over your lives and marriage.

Moreover, prayer strengthens the bond between you, joining together in seeking God's wisdom and direction for your marriage. By praying together regularly, you invite God to be the center of your relationship, inviting His love, grace, and power to transform your hearts and minds. In Matthew 18:20, Jesus promises, *"For where two or three gather in my name, there am I with them"* (NIV). As you come together in prayer, you experience the presence and power of God working in your midst, strengthening your bond, and deepening your faith.

> *Prayer is the cornerstone of a Christ–centered marriage, as it invites God's presence, guidance, and blessing into the relationship.*

Faith is the bedrock upon which a Christ–centered marriage is built, as it anchors the relationship in God's promises and truths.

Faith serves as the bedrock of a Christ–centered marriage by providing a solid foundation rooted in trust and commitment to God's principles.

Here's how it plays a crucial role:

- *Shared beliefs and values:* Faith establishes a common ground of shared beliefs and values between spouses, promoting unity and alignment in your spiritual journey.
- *Guidance and wisdom*: Faith offers guidance and wisdom through prayer, Scripture, and spiritual teachings, helping couples navigate challenges and decisions with divine insight.
- Strength in trials: During difficult times, faith provides resilience and hope, anchoring the marriage in God's promises and sustaining them through adversity.
- *Forgiveness and grac*e: Central to the Christian faith is the practice of forgiveness and extending grace to one another, which promotes humility, reconciliation, and growth within the marriage.
- *Purpose and direction*: Faith gives you a higher purpose and direction, helping you to prioritize God's will in your relationship and align your goals with His plan for your lives and marriage.

In essence, faith in Christ forms the bedrock of a marriage by nurturing spiritual growth, resilience, and a deep-seated commitment to honor God in all aspects of your relationship.

Hebrews 11:6 is a reminder that *"without faith, it is impossible to please God because anyone who comes to him must believe that he exists and that he rewards those who earnestly seek him"* (NIV). By cultivating a strong faith in God's love, provision, and faithfulness, you can weather the storms of life with courage, hope, and perseverance.

Furthermore, faith empowers you to navigate challenges and conflicts with grace and humility, trusting in God's grace and mercy to sustain you.

Faith empowers couples to navigate challenges and conflicts with grace and humility by fostering trust in God's guidance and provision. Here's how it works:

- *Trust in God's plan*: Faith encourages spouses to trust in God's sovereignty and wisdom, believing He has a purpose in every trial and conflict you will face.
- *Humility in relationships*: Faith promotes humility by reminding you of your own imperfections and the need to extend grace to one another as God extends grace to you.
- *Guidance through prayer*: Faith encourages you to seek God's guidance through prayer, asking for wisdom and discernment in resolving conflicts and making decisions.
- *Strengthening relationships*: Faith emphasizes the importance of forgiveness and reconciliation, helping to overcome conflicts and strengthen relationship bonds.
- *Resilience and hope*: Faith provides resilience by instilling hope in God's promises, even in challenging times, and believing that God can work all things together for your good.

Faith empowers you to navigate challenges and conflicts with grace and humility by relying on God's guidance, practicing forgiveness, and maintaining hope in His plan for your marriage. As you grow in your faith together, you become more attuned to God's leading and guidance in your marriage, making decisions that honor Him and reflect His love and truth.

Strengthening a Christ-centered marriage through prayer and faith is essential for nurturing a relationship that honors God and reflects His love and grace. By prioritizing prayer and cultivating a deep and abiding faith in God, you can experience the fullness of His blessings and presence in your marriage, creating a union that is grounded in love, unity, and purpose.

INVESTING IN THE RELATIONSHIP FOR THE LONG TERM

Building a strong foundation for your marriage involves investing in it for the long term, and a significant aspect of this investment is found in the power of your words. Words have the profound ability to either bless or curse, to build up or tear down, within the context of marriage. Proverbs 18:21 affirms this truth: *"The tongue has the power of life and death, and those who love it will eat its fruit"* (NIV).

In your marriage, the words you choose to speak can shape your home's atmosphere and your spouse's emotional well-being. Choosing words that affirm, encourage, and uplift strengthens the marital bond and fosters emotional intimacy. Conversely, words spoken in anger, criticism, or indifference can erode trust and create distance between the two of you.

As you consider investing in your relationships for the long term, it's vital to cultivate a habit of speaking words that reflect God's love and grace.

Every interaction in marriage provides an opportunity to speak blessings over each other. When you intentionally choose words that affirm your spouse's worth, express gratitude, and offer encouragement, you contribute to a positive marital environment. This aligns with biblical principles that emphasize love, kindness, and mutual respect as foundational to Christ-centered marriages.

Scripture teaches that the words you speak are reflective of your heart and have the power to shape your reality. Psalm 19:14 encourages you to pray, *"May these words of my mouth and this meditation of my heart be pleasing in your sight, Lord, my Rock and my Redeemer"* (NIV). By aligning your words with God's truth and love, you honor His design for marriage and contribute to its lasting strength.

By intentionally investing in positive communication habits and aligning your words with biblical principles, you not only strengthen your marriage but also reflect God's love and grace to your spouse and to the world around you.

In the spiritual realm, your words hold immense significance. They are not just expressions of your thoughts but can also shape reality and impact the atmosphere of your relationships. Proverbs 12:18 says, *"The words of the reckless pierce like swords, but the tongue of the wise brings healing"* (NIV). This verse underscores the dual nature of your words—they can wound deeply or bring healing and restoration.

As followers of Christ, your speech should reflect the character of God. Colossians 4:6 exhorts you, *"Let your conversation be always full of grace, seasoned with salt, so that you may know how to answer everyone"* (NIV). Words should be seasoned with grace, reflecting God's love, mercy, and truth. When you speak from a place of humility and love, your words can minister to the heart of your spouse as no one else can and build them up in their faith and identity in Christ. Is this a foreign concept for you? Have you ever wondered who you are in Christ? As a believer in Christ, your identity is who Christ says you are. (Please refer to the **52 WEEKLY AFFIRMATIONS OF YOUR IDENTITY IN CHRIST**, which can be found in the Resource section at the back of the book, for a list of who you are in Christ.)

Ephesians 4:29 provides further guidance on the use of your words: *"Do not let any unwholesome talk come out of your mouths, but only what is helpful for building others up according to their needs, that it may benefit those who listen"* (NIV). This verse challenges you to consider the impact of your words on others, especially within the sacred covenant of marriage.

Are your words nurturing and affirming, or do they tear down and cause harm?

In marriage, the power of your words can influence your relationship's emotional climate and spiritual health. You create a positive atmosphere where love and trust can thrive when you speak words of affirmation, appreciation, and encouragement. Conversely, negative words, such as criticism, blame, or harshness, can create barriers to intimacy and erode the foundation of mutual respect and understanding.

Jesus Himself emphasized the importance of your words in Matthew 12:36-37, *"But I tell you that everyone will have to give account on the day of judgment for every empty word they have spoken. For by your words, you will be acquitted, and by your words, you will be condemned"* (NIV). These words remind us of the weightiness of speech and the need to steward our words wisely, especially in the context of marriage, where hearts are bonded by a sacred vow before God and to each other.

As you strive to align your words with God's truth and love, you participate in His redemptive work within your marriage. Words can convey forgiveness, reconciliation, and hope, pointing your spouse toward Christ and His transformative power. By embracing the spiritual significance of your words, you honor God's design for marriage and contribute to its growth and flourishing as a reflection of His glory.

Here are some affirmations to declare God's goodness over yourself, your spouse, your marriage, and your family:

- I am too blessed to be stressed.
- I am too blessed to be depressed.
- My setbacks prepare me for my comeback.
- I will transform my mess into a message.
- My test will become my testimony.
- I am too joyful to be fearful.

Have fun embracing these affirmations. You are choosing to focus on the abundant blessings and positive outcomes that God has promised. By declaring these truths over your life and relationships, you invite His goodness to manifest in every aspect.

This practice not only nurtures a heart of gratitude and resilience but also strengthens the bond between you and your loved ones. Remember, as you speak these words of faith and encouragement, you align your heart with God's vision, cultivating a strong and enduring marriage and family life that radiates His love and grace.

Embracing the powerful proclamations that celebrate God's goodness and your blessings sets a positive tone for nurturing your marriage. As you speak these affirmations over your life and relationship, you are building a foundation of faith and gratitude that fuels your commitment to one another. By investing in your relationship for the long term, it is essential to cultivate a strong and enduring marriage that withstands the test of time and grows stronger with each passing year. This involves more intentional actions and commitments that foster a deep and resilient bond, allowing your marriage to flourish amidst life's challenges.

Here's how to do it:

- *Commitment*: Commit to prioritizing your relationship over time, making it a central focus in your life.
- *Communication*: Foster open and honest communication, ensuring both partners feel heard, understood, and valued.
- *Quality time*: Dedicate regular quality time together, nurturing your emotional connection and intimacy.
- *Shared goals*: Establish and work towards shared goals, both personal and relational, fostering mutual growth and alignment.
- *Conflict resolution*: Learn and practice healthy conflict resolution skills, addressing issues promptly and constructively.
- *Continuous learning*: Invest in personal growth and learning together, exploring new interests, and evolving as individuals and as a couple.
- *Support and encouragement*: Provide mutual support and encouragement, celebrate successes, and offer comfort in challenges.
- *Spiritual connection*: Foster a shared spiritual foundation, seeking God's guidance and wisdom in your relationship.

By consistently investing in these areas, couples can cultivate a marriage that not only survives but thrives, growing stronger and deeper with each passing year.

This investment involves your intentional efforts, sacrifices, and commitments to nurture and sustain the marital bond, creating a foundation of love, trust, and mutual support that stands firm amidst life's challenges.

One of the key aspects of investing in long-term relationships is prioritizing quality time together. In the hustle and bustle of everyday life, you can easily become caught up in your individual responsibilities and neglect your relationship.

However, setting aside dedicated time for each other allows you to connect, communicate, and deepen your bond, strengthening the foundation of your marriage. Whether through regular date nights, weekend getaways, or simply spending quiet evenings at home, prioritizing quality time together furthers intimacy, connection, and joy within the marital relationship.

Additionally, investing in the relationship for the long term involves continuous growth and personal development. As an individual and as a couple, you should be committed to learning, growing, and evolving together, both personally and relationally.

This may involve attending marriage enrichment programs, seeking counseling when needed, or reading books and articles on relationships and communication. By investing in personal growth and relational skills, you can navigate challenges more effectively, deepen your understanding of each other, and strengthen the overall health of your marriage.

Furthermore, investing in the relationship for the long term requires a commitment to open communication, honesty, and vulnerability. Creating a safe and supportive environment where you can share your thoughts, feelings, and concerns openly and honestly with each other is a must. This communication nurtures trust, understanding, and intimacy within the marriage, allowing you to navigate conflicts, resolve differences, and grow closer together over time.

Ultimately, investing in the relationship for the long term is a journey of love, dedication, and commitment that requires ongoing effort and intentionality from both of you. By prioritizing quality time together, cultivating personal growth and development, and nurturing open communication and trust, you can build a marriage that endures the trials of life and flourishes in the joy of shared love and companionship.

In my experience, marriages do not flourish when burdened by secrets—hiding issues that cry out for healing. Childhood traumas, painful break-ups, and words that haunt us through addiction and other struggles must be brought into the light and surrendered to Jesus for healing.

Fear thrives in darkness, but faith grows in the light of God's truth. Trusting in God nourishes what will thrive and leaves the rest to be covered by the redeeming grace of Jesus.

Ultimately, celebrating 1, 5, 10, 40, 50 years, and everything in between of marriage is a testament to the love, commitment, and dedication to you as a couple. By investing in your relationship through meaningful gestures, shared experiences, and spiritual growth, you can honor your journey together and look forward to many more years of love and happiness.

Take the necessary steps. Growth often involves discomfort, but freedom brings joy!

Practical Exercises

What commitments are you willing to make to support each other in achieving the goals you set during these exercises? Place a checkmark in the boxes you will commit to.

- ♡ **Renewing vows:** A vow renewal ceremony is a beautiful way to reaffirm your commitment to each other and celebrate their milestones together. Whether a simple ceremony at home or a lavish affair with family and friends, renewing vows can be a deeply meaningful and symbolic gesture of love and devotion. (**MARRIAGE RENEWAL VOWS** can be found in the Resources section at the back of this book.)

- ♡ **Reflecting on memories:** You can take time to reminisce and reflect on the memories you have shared over the years. Looking through old photo albums, watching wedding videos, or revisiting special places can evoke nostalgia and remind you of the journey you have been on together, strengthening your connection and appreciation for each other.

- ♡ **Planning a special getaway:** A romantic getaway can provide you with the opportunity to reconnect and rejuvenate the relationship. Whether it is a weekend retreat to a cozy bed and breakfast or a dream vacation to a tropical destination, spending quality time together away from the distractions of everyday life can reignite the spark and passion in your marriage.

- ♡ **Giving thoughtful gifts:** Thoughtful gifts that are meaningful and personalized can show spouses how much they are loved and appreciated. Whether it is a piece of jewelry, a handwritten love letter, or a custom-made keepsake, giving gifts that reflect the depth of your relationship can create cherished memories and strengthen your bond.

- ♡ **Engaging in shared activities:** You can celebrate your milestone anniversary by engaging in activities you both enjoy and cherish. Whether it is taking dance lessons together, going on a hiking adventure, or learning a new hobby, participating in shared activities can create lasting memories and deepen the connection between spouses.

- ♡ **Serving others together:** Volunteering or giving back to the community as a couple can be a meaningful way to celebrate a milestone anniversary. Whether it is serving at a local soup kitchen, participating in a charity event, or supporting a cause you are passionate about, you can strengthen your bond by making a positive impact on others' lives together.

- **Seeking spiritual guidance:** You can invest in your relationship by seeking spiritual guidance and support from your faith community. Whether attending marriage enrichment programs, participating in Bible studies, or seeking counseling from a pastor, you can deepen your faith and strengthen your relationship by learning and incorporating spiritual practices into your marriage.

How will you prioritize and allocate time in your schedule to work on the practical exercises in this chapter together as a couple?

_____

_____

_____

_____

_____

How will you measure and celebrate your progress?

_____

_____

_____

_____

_____

_____

_____

Reflection Questions

How do you currently prioritize investing in your relationship for the long term?

_____
_____
_____
_____

What activities or practices have been most beneficial in nurturing your bond and strengthening your connection?

_____
_____
_____
_____

How can you continue to prioritize and sustain your investment in your relationship for the long term, even amidst the busyness of life?

_____
_____
_____
_____

CHAPTER SEVEN

OVERCOMING CHALLENGES TOGETHER

"Two are better than one, because they have a good return for their labor: If either of them falls down, one can help the other up. But pity anyone who falls and has no one to help them up. Also, if two lie down together, they will keep warm. But how can one keep warm alone? Though one may be overpowered, two can defend themselves."

~ Ecclesiastes 4:9-11 (NIV)

In every marriage, challenges are inevitable – whether they stem from external pressures, communication breakdowns, or personal struggles. However, how you navigate these challenges together defines the strength and resilience of your relationship. Take the time you need to contemplate these strategies and principles that will empower you to overcome challenges with grace, unity, and faith.

Addressing common challenges together is a hallmark of a healthy and thriving marriage. From financial stress and parenting disagreements to conflicts in communication and intimacy, you must confront these issues head-on, seeking solutions and compromises that honor your relationship and individual needs. By promoting open communication, empathy, and teamwork, you can navigate challenges with a sense of solidarity and mutual support, strengthening your bond in the process.

It's important to recognize and preserve your individual identities within the marital relationship. Doing this can turn obstacles into stepping stones to help overcome challenges when they arise. When both partners maintain their sense of self—beyond their role as a spouse—it breeds personal growth and fulfillment. Recognizing that each of you is a complete individual with unique gifts, talents, plans, and purposes allows you to contribute more fully to the marriage while honoring your individuality.

Dealing with external pressures and influences is another significant aspect of overcoming challenges together. In a world filled with distractions, temptations, and competing priorities, you must unite against external forces that threaten to undermine your relationship. Whether it is societal expectations, family dynamics, or cultural norms, you can lean on each other for strength and resilience, remaining steadfast in your commitment to one another and shared values.

Seeking Godly counsel is critical for you when facing challenges in your marriage. As believers, you can turn to God in prayer, seeking His wisdom, comfort, and guidance in times of trial. Additionally, seeking support—whether it is through biblical counseling, mentorship, or accountability groups—can provide you with the encouragement, resources, and spiritual insight you need to overcome challenges and grow closer to God and each other. There is no shame in seeking help. God has raised up godly counselors to bring healing, lifting off the band-aid to reveal the reason for the hurt.

There was a time in my marriage when I thought we would not make it. I had been hiding every need to myself and not allowing anyone to help me. This was reflected in one of my precious children, who needed counseling during their teenage years. Eventually, I was brought into the healing process to find out I needed my own healing. I was so shut off that I created an unhealthy boundary of not needing anyone.

During one of my sessions, I blurted out I wanted to separate from my husband. The pain of seeing my child suffering, the hurt I felt from childhood, and my marriage falling apart was all too much for me to bear. I simply wanted to run away, give up, and leave it for God to handle.

The problem was the problem. I was not the problem. I needed a solution. My counselor told me flat out that I did not need a separation. I needed to learn how to make it work. She was so right. My natural way of thinking is to find a solution to each problem, which is good until I have to put the human part into the equation. I needed to feel what my loved ones were feeling, but I also needed to feel what I was feeling. I lived on the back burner of life. I did this most of my young life and brought it into my marriage. Do not ask for help; do it yourself; you do not need anyone. The gift I had in my husband was not realized until I decided that I was going to be "all in" for our marriage instead of running away. I began changing my thoughts, walking closer to Jesus each day, and believing in God, not just believing in Him. This is a mighty work still going on in my not "so young" life.

The themes of addressing common challenges together, dealing with external pressures and influences, and seeking guidance and support from God and the Christian community are inspired to confront challenges with faith, resilience, and unity. Together, you can embrace the journey of overcoming challenges as an opportunity to strengthen your marriage, deepen your trust in God, and experience the transformative power of love and grace within the sacred covenant of marriage.

ADDRESSING COMMON CHALLENGES FACED BY COUPLES

Addressing common challenges faced by couples is a crucial aspect of nurturing a healthy and thriving marriage. While every relationship is unique, you may encounter obstacles and struggles along your journey together. By acknowledging and addressing these challenges with open communication, empathy, and teamwork, you can strengthen your bond and navigate life's ups and downs with resilience and grace.

A common challenge is financial stress. Money-related conflicts, debt, and financial instability can place a strain on a marriage and create tension in your relationship. Setting clear financial goals, creating a budget, and working together to manage expenses and save for the future can alleviate financial stress and strengthen your financial foundation.

Additionally, fostering open communication about money, discussing financial priorities, and making joint decisions regarding spending and saving can help you navigate financial challenges with unity and mutual support.

Parenting disagreements are also a common challenge, especially as you navigate the joys and complexities of raising children together. Differences in parenting styles, discipline techniques, and family dynamics can lead to conflicts and tensions between spouses. By approaching parenting as a team, setting clear expectations, and communicating openly about parenting goals and values, you can work together to create a cohesive and supportive parenting approach that honors your family's unique dynamics.

Moreover, managing work-life balance and external pressures is a challenge that many of you face in today's fast-paced world. Balancing career demands, household responsibilities, and personal interests can leave you feeling overwhelmed and disconnected. By prioritizing quality time together, setting boundaries around work and technology, and supporting each other's personal and professional goals, you can cultivate a healthy work-life balance and strengthen your relationship.

Ultimately, addressing common challenges you face requires a commitment to open communication, mutual respect, and shared problem-solving. By facing challenges together as a team, you can deepen your bond, strengthen your relationship, and build a foundation of love, trust, and resilience that sustains you through life's journey.

DEALING WITH EXTERNAL PRESSURES AND INFLUENCES

Dealing with external pressures and influences is an inevitable part of married life as you navigate the complexities of the world around you while striving to maintain a strong and thriving relationship. External pressures and influences can come in various forms and may challenge the marriage's unity, harmony, and intimacy.

Understanding these external factors and learning to manage them effectively is essential to preserving your bond and upholding shared values and commitments.

One common external pressure you face is societal expectations and cultural norms. Society often imposes certain expectations and standards on relationships, marriage, and family life, which can pressure you to conform to these ideals. Whether it's societal pressure to have a certain lifestyle, achieve specific milestones, or conform to traditional gender roles, you may feel the weight of external expectations impacting your relationship.

By recognizing and discussing these societal pressures openly, you can affirm your values, priorities, and goals for your marriage rather than succumbing to external expectations that may not align with your vision for the relationship.

Family dynamics and relationships with extended family members can also be a source of external pressure for you. Conflicting expectations, interference, or unresolved issues within the extended family can create tension and strain on the marital relationship. You may struggle to establish boundaries, communicate effectively, or navigate differences in family cultures and traditions. By setting healthy boundaries, prioritizing open communication, and supporting each other as a united front, you can navigate family dynamics with grace and resilience, maintaining the integrity of marriage while honoring familial ties.

Moreover, external pressures may arise from career demands, financial stress, or societal trends that impact your daily lives and routines. Balancing work obligations, financial responsibilities, and personal pursuits can be challenging, particularly in today's fast-paced world. You may find yourself grappling with time constraints, competing priorities, or conflicts around work-life balance. By prioritizing open communication, setting shared goals, and supporting each other's individual aspirations, you can navigate external pressures related to career and finances with unity and mutual support, preserving the strength and stability of your marriage amidst life's demands.

Ultimately, dealing with external pressures and influences requires you to cultivate resilience, flexibility, and a strong sense of shared purpose and identity. By openly acknowledging and addressing external pressures, you can strengthen your bond, deepen your connection, and weather the challenges of married life with grace and resilience. It takes mutual support, understanding, and commitment to each other to overcome external pressures and influences to build a better marriage that stands the test of time.

SEEKING GUIDANCE AND SUPPORT FROM GOD AND THE CHRISTIAN COMMUNITY

Seeking guidance and support from God and the Christian community is integral to fostering a strong and resilient marriage built on a foundation of faith, love, and shared values. In the journey of marriage, you encounter various challenges, uncertainties, and complexities that may test your resolve and commitment to each other. By turning to God and seeking wisdom, strength, and guidance from Him, you can find solace, direction, and hope in the midst of life's trials.

God's Word provides you with timeless principles and truths that offer guidance and encouragement for navigating the complexities of married life. Through prayer, meditation on Scripture, and seeking discernment from the Holy Spirit, you can align your hearts and minds with God's will for your marriage, allowing His wisdom and grace to permeate every aspect of your relationship.

Perhaps you felt as I did when I thought I had all the answers but came up short.

Why?

God's will is perfect. Mine is not. Yours is not either. Trusting in the Lord is essential for overcoming challenges.

Proverbs 3:5-6 is a reminder to *"Trust in the Lord with all your heart and lean not on your own understanding; in all your ways submit to him, and he will make your paths straight"* (NIV). He has all the right solutions for your problems. By surrendering to God's plan and seeking His guidance, you can experience His peace and presence, guiding you through life's challenges and uncertainties.

> *Seeking guidance and support from God and the Christian community is integral to fostering a strong and resilient marriage built on a foundation of faith, love, and shared values.*

As Jim Rohn famously stated, *"You become like the company you keep,"* although this concept has earlier roots. The earliest reference can be found in Proverbs 13:20: "Whoever walks with the wise becomes wise, but the companion of fools will suffer harm" (ESV). Additionally, a similar sentiment appears in the work *Don Quixote de la Mancha*,[10] published in 1615. This notion emphasizes the profound effect of surrounding oneself with positive, godly influences. Seeking those who pray for you, speak blessings over your life, and offer godly counsel is crucial. Reflecting on past experiences, I have seen firsthand the effects of being around the wrong crowd, leading to regrettable actions and deeper repercussions than anticipated.

Moreover, seeking support from the Christian community provides you with a network of encouragement, accountability, and fellowship that strengthens your faith and sustains your marriage. *"As iron sharpens iron, so one person sharpens another"* (Proverbs 27:17 NIV).

Whether it is through participation in a local church, joining a small group or Bible study, or seeking mentorship from more experienced people, you can find a supportive community of believers who share their values, beliefs, and commitment to Christ. By surrounding yourself with fellow believers who can offer prayer, counsel, and support, you can find comfort and strength in knowing that you are not alone in your journey.

Seeking guidance and support from God and the Christian community is important because it reinforces the spiritual dimension of marriage, reminding you that your relationship is not solely dependent on your own strength or efforts but on the grace and power of God working in and through them. By nurturing a deep and abiding reliance on God and cultivating a supportive community of believers, you can weather the storms of life with faith, resilience, and unity, knowing that you are upheld by the love and grace of your Heavenly Father and supported by your Christian brothers and sisters.

Ultimately, seeking guidance and support from God and the Christian community strengthens your faith, deepens your relationship with each other, and anchors your marriage in the timeless truths and promises of God's Word. By embracing the spiritual dimension of marriage and leaning on the support of your Christian community, you can cultivate a marriage that honors God, reflects His love, and stands as a testament to His faithfulness and grace.

Practical Exercises

What specific actions will you commit to taking in order to complete the practical exercises in this chapter together as a team?

- ♡ Set aside dedicated time to identify and discuss common challenges or stressors that you face as a couple. Use open and honest communication to explore potential solutions and strategies for overcoming these challenges together.

- ♡ Create a plan of action that outlines specific steps you will take as a couple to address and overcome the challenges you have identified. Break down each step into manageable tasks and commit to supporting each other throughout the process.

- ♡ Develop boundaries and strategies for managing external pressures and influences as a couple. This may involve setting limits on work hours, prioritizing quality time together, or seeking support from trusted friends or family members.

How can you create a supportive environment that encourages both of you to engage in these exercises and remain accountable to one another?

What challenges do you foresee in implementing these exercises, and how will you address them to stay committed to your growth as a couple?

Reflection Questions

What are some common challenges or obstacles that you face as a couple, and how do they impact your relationship?

_____
_____
_____
_____
_____

What boundaries can you put in place to protect your relationship from outside stressors and distractions?

_____
_____
_____
_____
_____

How can you support each other in managing external pressures and staying focused on your marriage and faith?

_____
_____
_____
_____
_____

By engaging in these practical exercises and reflection questions, you can strengthen your bond, deepen your faith, and overcome challenges together with God's help and support from your Christian community.

CHAPTER EIGHT

EMBRACING GOD'S DESIGN FOR MARRIAGE

"If you want to enjoy life and see many happy days, keep your tongue from speaking evil and your lips from telling lies. Turn away from evil and do good. Search for peace, and work to maintain it."

~ 1 Peter 3: 10-11 (NLT)

*M*arriage is a sacred covenant ordained by God, designed to reflect His love, grace, and purpose for humanity. In this final chapter, we will gaze upon the profound beauty and purpose of marriage as envisioned by God, exploring how you can embrace His design and live out His plan for your relationship together. Through a Christ-centered marriage rooted in love, faith, and obedience to God's Word, you can leave a lasting legacy of love that honors God and impacts future generations.

Just think, an inheritance that lives on in others!

Celebrating the beauty and purpose of marriage by God's design is a testament to the divine wisdom and intentionality behind the marital union. From the beginning of creation, God ordained marriage as a sacred bond between a man and a woman, designed to reflect His image and bring glory to His name.

There was a time when I had to humble myself and ask my husband for forgiveness, even though I initially wanted to prove myself right. I had frequently taken on roles that rightfully belonged to him as the leader of our family. Witnessing the pain this caused him deeply affected me, and through the conviction of the Holy Spirit, I realized it was no longer about being right but about aligning with God's vision for our marriage and establishing healthy boundaries.

As your children observe these changes, they begin to see the transformative power of God's wisdom in your relationships, laying a foundation for a legacy of healing and strength.

Marriage's beauty lies in reconciliation. I faced a crucial choice: insist on being right or allow God to heal our marriage. It's not a one-time decision but a continual choice, especially when the enemy tries to steer you away from forgiveness to bitterness.

As you embrace the beauty of marriage as a gift from God, you discover the depth of His love and purpose for your relationship, finding joy and fulfillment in honoring His design for your lives.

Living out God's plan for marriage daily is a journey of faith, obedience, and surrender to His will. As you seek to align your heart and mind with God's Word, discover the transformative power of His love and grace working in and through your relationship.

By prioritizing prayer, studying Scripture, and seeking God's guidance in your daily decisions and interactions, you can experience the fullness of God's blessings and presence in marriage, finding strength and wisdom to navigate life's challenges and joys.

Through a healthy, strong, Christ-centered marriage, there is a lasting legacy that extends far beyond yourselves. As you cultivate a relationship rooted in love, faith, and obedience to God, you leave a powerful legacy of faithfulness, integrity, and love for future generations to emulate. Whether it's through raising children who follow God's ways, serving as mentors and role models to others, or impacting your community with acts of love and compassion, you can leave a lasting imprint on the world through your Christ-centered marriage.

As you explore celebrating the beauty and purpose of marriage, living out God's plan for marriage in daily life, and leaving a lasting legacy through a Christ-centered marriage, be inspired to embrace God's design for marriage wholeheartedly, trusting in His love, grace, and faithfulness to guide you on this sacred journey.

Together, we are committed to honoring God in your marriages, glorifying Him through your lives, and striving to leave a legacy of love that echoes throughout eternity.

CELEBRATING THE BEAUTY AND PURPOSE OF MARRIAGE

Recognizing the beauty and purpose in your marriage is a journey of discovery and deep connection. It begins with reflection—a deliberate pause to appreciate the journey you and your spouse have embarked upon together. Whether through shared milestones, overcoming challenges, or moments of joy, these experiences weave a tapestry reflecting your unique bond. Gratitude for these moments strengthens the foundation of your marriage, fostering resilience and appreciation for each other's presence in your lives.

Understanding the purpose of your marriage involves identifying shared goals and values. When you and your spouse align your aspirations with God's principles, your relationship becomes a vessel for mutual growth and fulfillment. This alignment guides your decisions and imbues your actions with a sense of purpose that extends beyond yourselves—to your family, community, and beyond.

Central to recognizing the beauty and purpose of your marriage is a commitment to open communication and spiritual connection. You deepen your understanding of God's plan for your union through heartfelt conversations and shared spiritual practices like prayer and study. This spiritual tie between you and God's Word nurtures a sense of unity and purpose, empowering you both to navigate life's challenges with faith and resilience. Studying and worshiping together in serving and supporting each other, you embody

God's love and grace, creating a legacy of enduring love and shared purpose that defines the beauty of your marriage.

Celebrating the beauty and purpose of marriage is a profound acknowledgment of the divine plan and intentionality behind the marital union. At its core, marriage is a sacred covenant ordained by God, designed to reflect His love, grace, and purpose for humanity. By recognizing and honoring the beauty and purpose of marriage, you can cultivate a deeper appreciation for the sanctity of your relationship and the profound blessings it brings into your lives.

Have you thought about what Heaven will be like? Why do I ask such a question? As you walk with God daily in your marriage, you will bring a bit of heaven to earth. Imagine the joy, celebrations, and peace there. I believe it is *Shalom*[11] to be experienced daily with intentional acts of love. It is the beauty and the mystery of marriage—the oneness of two imperfect people perfect together.

Here's how to celebrate the beauty and purpose of marriage:

One aspect of celebrating the beauty of marriage is recognizing it as a reflection of God's image and character. In Genesis 1:27-28, when God created man and woman in His own image and blessed them, He instructed them to be fruitful, multiply, and fill the earth. Marriage, therefore, serves as a tangible expression of God's love, unity, and creativity as you join together in a sacred bond that mirrors the unity and oneness of the Trinity.

Celebrating the beauty of marriage involves cherishing the unique qualities and characteristics of each spouse. In Ephesians 5:25-33, husbands are called to love their wives as Christ loved the church, and wives are called to respect and submit to their husbands. This mutual love, honor, and selflessness exemplify the beauty of marriage, which is a "togethership" grounded in love, respect, and mutual support.

Additionally, celebrating the purpose of marriage involves recognizing its role in fulfilling God's plan for human flourishing and redemption. Throughout Scripture, marriage is depicted as a covenant relationship designed to provide companionship, support, and partnership for you as you navigate life's joys and challenges together. As partners in God's kingdom, you are called to glorify Him through your marriage, reflecting His love, grace, and truth to the world around you.

Furthermore, celebrating the beauty and purpose of marriage entails embracing the sacredness of the marital bond and committing to its preservation and growth. By prioritizing intimacy, communication, and mutual respect, you can nurture a marriage that reflects the beauty of God's design and brings glory to His name. Through prayer, study of God's Word, and reliance on His wisdom and guidance, you can navigate the complexities of married life with faith, hope, and resilience, knowing that your union is part of God's divine plan for your lives.

Ultimately, celebrating the beauty and purpose of marriage is a lifelong journey of love, growth, and devotion. As you seek to honor God in your relationship, you'll leave a legacy of faithfulness and love for future generations. By embracing the sacredness of marriage and committing to its flourishing, you can experience the fullness of God's blessings and grace in your lives, rejoicing in the profound beauty and purpose of the marital union.

LIVING OUT GOD'S PLAN FOR MARRIAGE IN DAILY LIFE

Living out God's plan for marriage in daily life is a sacred calling and a sincere responsibility that requires you to align your heart and actions with the principles and values outlined in God's Word.

Building a strong foundation for your marriage rooted in God's Word involves several core principles. First, commit to daily devotions and prayer together, seeking God's wisdom and guidance. This habit strengthens your spiritual connection and helps you get through the challenges with faith and unity. Open and respectful communication is crucial—talk openly about your feelings, concerns, and dreams, fostering understanding and trust. Embrace forgiveness and grace, mirroring Christ's love for us by extending patience and compassion to each other in moments of conflict.

Shared values and goals rooted in biblical principles provide direction and purpose in your marriage journey. Establish priorities such as serving one another sacrificially and nurturing a spirit of humility and forgiveness. This foundation supports a loving and resilient relationship that honors God's plan for marriage. Engage with a supportive Christian community for encouragement and accountability, surrounding yourselves with mentors who uphold biblical values. Together, steward your resources wisely—time, finances, and talents—aligning them with God's purposes for your family's well-being and His glory.

Living out these principles every day can really transform your marriage into a reflection of God's love and grace. It strengthens your bond, equipping you to face challenges with resilience and mutual support. By prioritizing faith, communication, forgiveness, and shared values, you build a marriage that not only endures but also thrives—a testament to God's design for lifelong love and togetherness.

Daily habits and routines aligned with God's marriage plan are crucial for several reasons. Firstly, they provide a consistent framework for living out biblical principles and values in daily life. Starting each day with prayer, Scripture reading, and reflection reinforces your commitment to God and each other, fostering spiritual growth and unity.

Small, intentional actions such as regular communication, acts of kindness, and shared prayer times build trust and intimacy over time. These actions create a positive atmosphere where conflicts can be resolved with grace and forgiveness, reflecting Christ's love in the marriage. Consistent habits also help you stay focused on your shared goals and values, promoting unity and mutual support.

Moreover, aligning daily habits with God's marriage plan strengthens resilience during challenges. By relying on faith and biblical wisdom in decision-making and problem-solving, you develop a deeper trust in God's guidance and provision. This trust not only enhances the spiritual bond between each of you but also nurtures a resilient foundation that withstands the test of time.

In essence, daily habits and routines rooted in God's marriage plan transform individual actions into powerful tools for building and sustaining a healthy, Christ-centered marriage. Each small step taken in faith and obedience contributes to the overall health and strength of the relationship, allowing you to experience the abundant blessings of God's design for marriage.

I use a morning routine to help with being consistent and intentional. You may have heard of others using a similar routine. I call mine "8 before 8."[12] Here's an example of a morning routine designed to help you align with the principles of a Christ-centered marriage, focusing on spiritual growth, communication, and unity:

1. *Wake up early*: Start your day with intentionality and peace, making your bed.
2. *Prayer and devotion*: Begin with prayer together, committing your day and marriage to God. Read a passage of Scripture or a daily devotion that strengthens your faith and unity (e.g., Ephesians 5:21-33).
3. *Gratitude practice*: Take a moment to express gratitude individually and as a couple for blessings and each other. This fosters positivity and appreciation.
4. *Communication check-in*: Discuss any plans or concerns for the day ahead. Share your feelings and dreams openly, ensuring alignment and understanding (e.g., James 1:19).
5. *Physical activity*: Engage in light exercise together—whether it's a morning walk, stretching, or a short workout—to promote physical health and bond as a couple.
6. *Healthy breakfast*: Prepare and enjoy a nutritious breakfast together. Use this time to connect and plan for the day ahead.
7. *Personal growth*: Spend a few minutes individually on personal growth activities such as reading, journaling, or listening to uplifting podcasts that align with your values and goals.
8. *Reflection and affirmation*: End with a brief reflection on your morning routine and affirm each other's strengths and commitments. Pray for continued strength and guidance throughout the day.

Implementing these steps before 8 a.m. creates a solid foundation for your day and marriage, reinforcing spiritual growth, communication, and mutual support.

At its core, God's plan for marriage is rooted in love, faithfulness, and selflessness as you seek to honor God and reflect His image through your relationship. By embracing God's plan for marriage and applying it to your daily lives, you can experience the fullness of God's blessings and grace in your marriage.

The plan for marriage, as outlined in Scripture, is characterized by several key principles and values that guide you in your journey together. First and foremost, marriage is intended to be a lifelong covenant between a man and a woman, rooted in love, commitment, and mutual respect (Genesis 2:24). This covenant relationship reflects the unbreakable bond between Christ and His church, as husbands and wives are called to love and honor each other as Christ loves and cherishes His bride, the church (Ephesians 5:22-33).

Furthermore, God's plan for marriage emphasizes the importance of unity, servanthood, and mutual support between you. In marriage, you are called to become "one flesh," joining together in a sacred bond that transcends individuality and selfishness (Genesis 2:24). This unity is characterized by shared goals, shared values, and shared responsibilities as you work together to build a life that honors God and furthers His kingdom purposes.

Additionally, God's plan for marriage involves cultivating intimacy, communication, and vulnerability within the marital relationship. You are called to prioritize your relationship, make time for each other, listen to each other's needs, and nurture emotional and spiritual connection (1 Corinthians 7:3-5). Through open communication, honesty, and transparency, you can deepen your bond and strengthen your commitment to each other, fostering a relationship that reflects the love and grace of God.

Moreover, God's plan for marriage encompasses the roles and responsibilities of a husband and wife within the marital union. As a husband, you are called to love your wife sacrificially, leading with humility, compassion, and selflessness (Ephesians 5:25-29). As a wife, you are called to respect and submit to your husband, supporting and affirming his leadership in the marriage (Ephesians 5:22-24). Together, you are called to serve and honor each other, modeling Christ-like love and humility in your relationship.

Living out God's plan for marriage in daily life involves applying these principles and values to every aspect of the marital relationship. From communication and conflict resolution to intimacy and parenting, you are called to seek God's guidance and wisdom in all you do, trusting in His faithfulness to sustain and strengthen your marriage. By embracing God's plan for marriage and committing to live it out each day, you can experience the joy, fulfillment, and blessings that come from walking in obedience to God's Word.

LEAVING A LASTING LEGACY OF LOVE

In the mystery of life, you are marked by a beginning and an end, with a dash between. It's the dash[13] that defines your journey on earth and is a testament to how you lived, loved, and impacted others during your time here. (***THE DASH*** poem can be found in the Resources section at the back of this book.) While cherished memories are forgotten and pictures fade over time, the impact of loving well leaves an enduring imprint on hearts and lives, shaping the legacy we leave behind. How do you want to be remembered?

If your life here on this earth has never been just about you, then what is your place in history? What can you possibly leave for those who come after you?

What would go underneath the beginning and ending dates with the dash in between on your tombstone? What will your legacy be if your life on this earth has always been about more than just yourself? What will you leave behind for those who follow after you?

As I enter my later years, I reflect on what the dash between the dates on my tombstone should represent. If I could reflect on one thing, it would simply be this:

"She loved well."

Leaving a lasting legacy of love is to love well!

A lasting legacy of love is an aspiration for you who seek to honor God and impact future generations through your life, relationships, and marriage. It involves intentionally cultivating a relationship that reflects God's love, grace, and truth, leaving a positive imprint on your children, grandchildren, and beyond.

Write down your birth date, then add a dash. Spend time in prayer, considering how you want to be remembered. Now, begin planning from the perspective of leaving behind a lasting legacy of love.

Here's how you can start to leave a lasting legacy of love:

Leave a lasting legacy of love by modeling Christ-like love and selflessness in your relationship. This involves sacrificially serving and loving one another, putting each other's needs above your own, and demonstrating grace and forgiveness in times of conflict.

Establish and prioritize family values that reflect your commitment to God and His principles. These values may include integrity, honesty, compassion, and generosity, which are the foundation for a healthy and thriving family life.

Invest time, energy, and resources in building strong relationships with your children, grandchildren, and extended family members. This involves

> *Leave a lasting legacy of love by modeling Christ-like love and selflessness in your relationship*

spending quality time together, fostering open communication, and creating cherished memories that will be treasured for years to come.

You can pass down biblical truths and principles to the next generation, equipping your children and grandchildren with a strong foundation of faith and values. This may involve reading and studying the Bible together, praying as a family, and engaging in meaningful discussions about God's Word and His plan for your lives.

Be the one who brings peace into your marriage by being Christ-like in the most difficult of times, establishing biblical joy, and cultivating happiness along the way.

Serve others to make a positive impact in your family first, then your community. This may involve volunteering together, supporting charitable causes, and extending acts of kindness and compassion to those in need.

Pray for God's blessing, guidance, and protection over your children, grandchildren, and future generations. By committing your family to God in prayer, you can trust in His faithfulness to fulfill His purposes and plans for your family's legacy.

You can live with purpose and intentionality, seeking to glorify God in all you do and leaving a legacy that reflects His love and grace. This involves making decisions that align with your values and priorities and striving to live out your faith authentically in your daily life together.

By intentionally living out these principles and values, you can leave a lasting legacy of love that reflects God's goodness, grace, and faithfulness to future generations. As you invest in your relationship, prioritize your family, and seek to honor God in all you do, you can leave behind a legacy that brings glory to God and inspires others to follow in your footsteps of love and faith.

Your life can be characterized as someone "who loved well."

Here's how you can help connect the past with the future:

Create a family scrapbook or digital archive that preserves memories, photographs, and stories from your relationship and family life. By documenting your history, you can pass down cherished memories and traditions to future generations, fostering a sense of connection and belonging.

Establish meaningful family traditions that celebrate your values, faith, and heritage. Whether it's a weekly family dinner, an annual vacation, or a special holiday tradition, these rituals provide opportunities for bonding, reflection, and connection across generations.

Serve as a mentor and role model to offer others guidance, support, and encouragement as you navigate your own marital journey. By sharing your experiences, insights, and wisdom, you can empower others to build strong, healthy, and Christ–centered marriages.

Invest in the education and spiritual development of your children and grandchildren, supporting them in their academic pursuits and nurturing their faith through Christian education and discipleship programs. By prioritizing education, you can equip future generations with the knowledge, skills, and values they need to succeed in life.

Work together to create a family mission statement that articulates shared values, goals, and aspirations. This statement serves as a guiding framework for decision-making and provides a sense of purpose and direction for the family as you seek to honor God and live out your faith in daily life.

You can share personal testimonies of God's faithfulness, provision, and grace in your life, both individually and as a couple. By sharing your stories of redemption, healing, and restoration, you can inspire others to trust in God's faithfulness and experience His love in your own lives.

Establish a family prayer wall, journal, or group text where family members can write down prayer requests, answered prayers, and words of encouragement. This interactive display serves as a visual reminder of God's faithfulness and fosters a culture of prayer and intercession within the family.

By incorporating these practices into your daily lives, you can leave a lasting legacy of love that reflects your faith, values, and commitment to honoring God in your marriage and family life. Through intentional investment, creative expression, and faithful stewardship of relationships, you can make a lasting impact that extends far beyond your lifetime.

Building a Christ–centered marriage by God's design is essential for creating relationships that will last. Throughout this journey, you have explored the foundational principles of marriage as outlined in Scripture, including unity, mutual love, respect, fruitfulness, multiplication, and foundation in Christ. These pillars serve as the bedrock upon which strong, enduring marriages are built.

By prioritizing unity, you can forge a deep bond of oneness that transcends individual differences and challenges. Through mutual love and respect, you can honor and cherish one another, reflecting Christ's sacrificial love in your relationship.

Embracing fruitfulness and multiplication, you can cultivate a legacy of love, faith, and service that extends beyond themselves and impacts future generations. By anchoring your marriage in Christ, you can experience His presence and guidance as you navigate the ups and downs of life together.

Ultimately, the importance of building a Christ–centered marriage by God's design cannot be overstated. Such marriages are marked by love, joy, and resilience, even in the face of adversity. They serve as a testament to the transformative power of faith and the enduring strength of God's design for marriage. As you commit to walking in obedience to God's Word and following His plan for your relationship, you can experience the fullness of His blessings and the joy of a love that lasts a lifetime.

May you strive to build Christ-centered marriages that glorify God, honor one another, and stand as a beacon of hope and inspiration to the world. With God at the center of your relationships, you can be confident that your marriages will not only endure but thrive, bringing glory to His name for generations to come.

Practical Exercises

Which of the following exercises are you willing to commit to? Please check the corresponding box for your choice.

- ♡ **Celebrating the Beauty and Purpose of Marriage:** Plan a special date night or weekend getaway to celebrate your marriage and reflect on the beauty and purpose of your relationship. Take time to reminisce about your journey together, expressing gratitude for how God has blessed and sustained your marriage.

- ♡ **Living Out God's Plan for Marriage in Daily Life:** Commit to incorporating daily habits and practices that align with God's design for marriage. Set aside time each day for prayer, Bible reading, and spiritual reflection as a couple, seeking God's guidance and wisdom in all aspects of your relationship.

- ♡ **Through a Healthy, Strong, Christ-centered marriage, there is a lasting legacy:** Reflect on the legacy you want to leave for future generations through your marriage. Consider ways to invest in your relationship now to build a legacy of faith, love, and commitment that will endure for generations to come.

How will you actively incorporate the principles from this chapter into your daily lives to embrace God's design for your marriage?

What specific steps can you take to celebrate the beauty and purpose of your relationship, and how will you make this a regular practice?

In what ways do you envision your Christ-centered marriage leaving a lasting legacy, and how will you ensure that you are both committed to this goal?

Reflection Questions

What are some specific ways in which your marriage reflects the beauty and purpose of God's design?

_____

_____

_____

_____

How do your daily habits and routines reflect your commitment to living out God's plan for your marriage?

_____

_____

_____

_____

What legacy do you want to leave for future generations through your marriage?

_____

_____

_____

_____

YOUR JOURNEY CONTINUES

*Y*ou have come to the end of the book, but your journey continues.

As a wife, you are called to respect and submit to your husband, affirming and supporting his leadership in the marriage. Each day is a gift to hold dearly close to your heart. Going through life together and learning from your time together will help you to be better and to have a better marriage with Christ in the center.

As a husband, remember that you are the spiritual leader and protector of your home, called by God to love your wife with the same sacrificial love Christ has for the Church. Your words and actions can build her up, strengthen her faith, and create an environment where she can flourish. In every season of your marriage, stay committed to honoring her, listening with empathy, and showing grace in times of struggle. Lead with humility and patience, knowing that your example shapes your relationship. By consistently placing Christ at the center of your marriage, you build a foundation that honors God and leaves a lasting legacy of love, trust, and faith for future generations.

It is a journey to building a Christ-centered marriage by God's design that encompasses a profound exploration of foundational principles and practical wisdom gleaned from Scripture. We began with forgiveness and grace, recognizing that grace is the bedrock of every healthy relationship. As we extend grace to one another, we emulate God's unconditional love and forgiveness, which form the cornerstone of marital harmony.

God's Design for Marriage: A Blueprint for Lasting Love in Christ provides you with the architectural framework upon which strong marriages are built. Just as a skilled architect meticulously plans each detail of a building, so too must you diligently align your lives with God's divine plan for marriage. This blueprint ensures that your union stands firm against life's storms and flourishes in God's intended purpose.

God's plan for marriage emphasizes the importance of seeking His wisdom in every aspect of marital life. By surrendering to His will and aligning with His Word, you discover the richness of His blessings and the guidance needed to navigate challenges with wisdom and discernment.

Effective communication is the lifeblood of every successful marriage. By learning to speak truth in love, listen actively, and resolve conflicts peacefully, you created an environment where trust and understanding thrive, deepening your emotional connection and unity.

Nurturing intimacy goes beyond physical affection; it involves cultivating emotional, spiritual, and relational closeness. Intimacy flourishes when you create a safe space to share your deepest desires, fears, and dreams, fostering a bond that strengthens your commitment and mutual respect.

Building a strong foundation requires intentional investment in spiritual growth, personal development, and shared values. By anchoring your marriage in Christ and prioritizing unity, love, and respect, you establish a solid foundation that withstands the test of time and trials.

Overcoming challenges together acknowledges that every marriage faces obstacles. Yet, by facing challenges united in faith, resilience, and mutual support, you will grow stronger together, learning from adversity and trusting in God's provision and grace.

Embracing God's design for marriage is a lifelong commitment to honoring God through your relationship. By embracing His design for marriage—rooted in sacrificial love, mutual submission, and selfless service—you reflect God's image to the world, becoming a testament to His faithfulness and grace.

As you journey through these foundational principles, you not only strengthen your own relationship but also leave a legacy of lasting love for future generations. The legacy of a Christ-centered marriage is an inheritance that outlasts the test of time, impacting children, grandchildren, and communities with the transformative power of God's love. By modeling faithfulness, grace, and steadfast commitment, you will inspire others to pursue God's design for marriage, creating a ripple effect of hope and healing in a world hungry for enduring love.

With these foundational principles, may you continually seek God's presence, guidance, and transformation in your life. May your marriage be a beacon of hope, a testament to God's love, and a blessing to each other and those around you. In building a Christ-centered marriage, let love, faith, and obedience to God's Word be your guiding light, ensuring that your union flourishes in His everlasting grace and purpose.

EMBRACING YOUR DREAM MARRIAGE

As you continue your journey toward the marriage you've always dreamed of, remember that it's a journey of growth, healing, and renewal. By unpacking emotional baggage and setting healthy boundaries, you lay the groundwork for a resilient, fulfilling, and lasting marriage—a true dream home for your hearts.

Just as a dream house requires ongoing maintenance and care, so does your marriage. Embrace the journey with courage, compassion, and a shared commitment to nurturing your relationship. Together, you can create a marriage as beautiful and enduring as the home of your dreams.

Spending this time with you has been a dream come true for me. Reflecting on our journey together, I am grateful for the moments we've shared, the lessons learned, and the growth that was experienced. Whether joyful or challenging, each step has brought you closer to the marriage you've always dreamed of. Just as a dream house is built with care, love, and dedication, so too is your relationship.

As you navigate life's seasons, cherish the memories, embrace the present, and look forward to the future with hope and faith. Thank you for being a part of this incredible journey. Together, with God's grace, you can build a love that stands the test of time.

RESOURCES

SALVATION PRAYER

Father God,

I now see that I am powerless to manage my life by myself. I am a sinner in need of saving. I've come to realize that I need to be restored to wholeness through Your Son, Jesus Christ.

I repent of my sins, and I ask Jesus to be my Lord and Savior. Please, come into my heart now. I want to be Yours. I have made a conscious decision to turn my entire life and will over to You, Jesus.

Thank you, Father God, for saving me through Your grace and mercy. I am a new creation!

Name_____ Date_____

FORGIVENESS PRAYER

(Matthew 6:9-14 NIV)

Heavenly Father,

I acknowledge my unforgiveness as a sinner; therefore, I come before you in the name of Jesus and by the power of the blood, and I choose to forgive (name) _____ for the sin of_____.

I ask to be healed of a broken heart, a body that is free from shame, anger, bitterness, and fear. I seek the renewing of my mind in this situation (Romans 12:1-2).

As an act of obedience, I release (name)_____ for what they did and cancel their debt to me.

I cancel all of Satan's authority over me because it has been forgiven.

Holy Spirit, I understand you may speak to me in a quiet voice, in a dream, through a vision, or take the pain and leave Your shalom. I seek Your truth for my healing.

In Jesus' name, I pray.[14]

What is the Holy Spirit revealing to you?

PRAYER OF ST. FRANCIS OF ASSISI

Lord, make me an instrument of Your peace;

Where there is hatred, let me sow love;

Where there is injury, pardon;

Where there is doubt, faith;

Where there is despair, hope;

Where there is darkness, light;

And where there is sadness, joy.

O Divine Master,

Grant that I may not so much seek

To be consoled as to console;

To be understood, as to understand;

To be loved, as to love;

For it is in giving that we receive,

It is in pardoning that we are pardoned,

And it is in dying that we are born to Eternal Life. Amen.[15]

THE SERENITY PRAYER

God, grant me the serenity

to accept the things I cannot change,

the courage to change the things I can,

and the wisdom to know the difference.

Living one day at a time,

enjoying one moment at a time,

enjoying hardship as a pathway to peace,

taking as Jesus did this sinful world as it is,

not as I would have it, trusting that You will make

all things right if I surrender to Your will;

so that I may be reasonably happy in this life

and supremely happy with You in the next.[16]

- Attributed to Reinhold Niebuhr

MARRIAGE PRAYER

Heavenly Father,

We come before you today with hearts full of gratitude for the gift of marriage. Thank you for bringing us together as husband and wife, united in love and commitment. As we embark on this journey together, we pray for your guidance and wisdom to lead us every step of the way.

Lord, help us always to keep you at the center of your marriage. May our love for each other be a reflection of your love for us, selfless, unconditional, and unwavering. Teach us to cherish and honor one another, to seek forgiveness and extend grace in times of weakness, and always to speak the truth in love.

Grant us the strength to weather the storms of life together, knowing that with you, all things are possible. Help us to face challenges with courage, celebrate joys with gratitude, and grow closer to each other and to you through every season of life.

Lord, we pray for unity in our marriage and that we may always be of one heart and one mind, supporting and encouraging each other in all we do. Give us the wisdom to make decisions that honor you and edify your relationship and the humility to seek guidance when we falter.

Father, bless your marriage with love that deepens with each passing day, with joy that overflows in times of abundance and in times of need, and with a bond that grows stronger with every trial we face. May our marriage be a testament to your faithfulness and grace, a beacon of light and hope to those around us.

We commit our marriage into your hands, Lord, trusting in your provision and protection. May your presence dwell richly in our home, filling it with peace, joy, and love. And may our union bring glory to your name, both now and forevermore.

In Jesus' name, we pray,

Amen.

MARRIAGE RENEWAL VOWS

FROM A MAN'S HEART TO HIS WIFE, WITH CHRIST AS THE CENTER

My dearest [Wife's Name],

As I stand before you today, I am filled with overwhelming gratitude for the gift of your love in my life. From the moment I first saw you, I knew that you were the one I wanted to spend forever with. Today, as we renew your vows, I want to express the depth of my love and commitment to you, with Christ as the center of our marriage.

I promise to cherish and honor you as Christ cherishes and honors His bride, the Church. I vow to be your rock, your shelter, and your support through every trial and triumph, seeking guidance from the Word of God. I pledge to love you unconditionally, with the love that Christ has shown to us, sacrificial and unconditional.

With every beat of my heart, I will strive to be the husband you deserve, seeking strength and wisdom from your Lord Jesus Christ. You are my partner and soulmate, and I am grateful for the privilege of sharing my life with you as we walk together on the path that God has laid before us.

I promise to be faithful to you in thought, word, and deed, with Christ as your example of love and faithfulness. With Him as our guide, I look forward to the journey ahead, knowing that with you by my side and Christ in our hearts, there is nothing we cannot overcome. I love you more than words can express, and I thank God every day for blessing me with your love. Today, tomorrow, and always, I am yours, completely and forever.

With all my love,

FROM A WOMAN'S HEART TO HER HUSBAND WITH CHRIST AS THE CENTER

My beloved [Husband's Name],

As we stand here together today, surrounded by the love of your family and friends, my heart overflows with gratitude for the gift of your love in my life. From the moment I met you, I knew that you were the one I had been waiting for, my partner and my confidant, with Christ as the center of our marriage.

Today, as we renew our vows, I want to take this opportunity to express the depth of my love and commitment to you, with Christ as our foundation. I promise to stand by your side through every twist and turn of life's journey, seeking guidance and strength from our Lord Jesus Christ.

I vow to be your faithful companion, your trusted ally, and your unwavering source of strength, with Christ as our example of love and sacrifice. I pledge to honor and respect you, to laugh with you in times of joy, and to hold you close in times of sorrow, drawing strength from your shared faith in Christ.

With every breath I take, I will cherish the bond we share, knowing that it is a gift from God to be treasured and nurtured. I promise to be your partner in every sense of the word, seeking wisdom and grace from our Lord Jesus Christ as we walk together in His footsteps.

I am grateful for the love you have shown me, for the sacrifices you have made, and for the joy you bring into my life each and every day. You are my rock, my hero, and my greatest blessing, and I am honored to call you my husband, with Christ as the center of our marriage. I love you now and always, and I look forward to growing old with you, hand in hand, heart to heart, forever and ever, with Christ as our guide and strength.

With all my love,

THE FOUR FOUNDATIONAL PILLARS OF GOD'S PROMISES

Faithfulness: God remains true to His Word and never breaks His promises.

Love: God's promises are rooted in His unconditional love for us.

Mercy: He extends compassion and forgiveness, even when we don't deserve it.

Grace: God freely gives us His blessings and favor, not because of our merit, but because of His generosity.

KEY SCRIPTURES FOR YOUR MARRIAGE

1. **BE FRUITFUL AND MULTIPLY**

   - Genesis 2:24, *"Therefore a man shall leave his father and his mother and hold fast to his wife, and they shall become one flesh"* (ESV).
   - Ephesians 5:31, *"For this reason a man will leave his father and mother and be united to his wife, and the two will become one flesh"* (NIV).
   - 1 Corinthians 7:3-4, *"The husband should fulfill his marital duty to his wife, and likewise the wife to her husband. The wife does not have authority over her own body but yields it to her husband. In the same way, the husband does not have authority over his own body but yields it to his wife"* (NIV).
   - Proverbs 18:22, *"He who finds a wife finds a good thing and obtains favor from the Lord"* (ESV).
   - Malachi 2:15 (b), *"And what does the one God seek? Godly offspring"* (NIV).

2. **BLUEPRINT FOR A CHRIST–CENTERED BIBLICAL MARRIAGE SCRIPTURES**

   - **Foundation on Christ:** Christ is the cornerstone of the marriage, individually and collectively surrendering to His Lordship and following His teachings (Ephesians 5:22-33).
   - **Sacred Covenant:** Recognizing marriage as a covenant before God, where spouses commit to love, honor, and cherish each other unconditionally, mirroring Christ's sacrificial love for the Church.
   - **Mutual Submission and Respect:** Both spouses submit to one another out of reverence for Christ, with husbands loving their wives sacrificially and wives respecting and supporting their husbands (Ephesians 5:21).
   - **Communication and Unity:** Practicing open, honest communication and striving for unity in decision-making, goals, and values (Ephesians 4:2-3).
   - **Intimacy and Oneness:** Cultivating intimacy on all levels—spiritual, emotional, and physical—and embracing the oneness of marriage, where two become one flesh (Genesis 2:24, 1 Corinthians 7:3-5).
   - **Fruitfulness and Multiplication:** Embracing the call to be fruitful and multiply not only physically through children but also spiritually through discipleship and service together (Genesis 1:28, Mark 10:6-9).

- **Grace and Forgiveness:** Extending grace and forgiveness to one another as Christ forgave you, resolving conflicts in a spirit of humility and reconciliation (Colossians 3:13, Ephesians 4:32).
- **Shared Spiritual Growth:** Pursuing individual and collective spiritual growth through prayer, Scripture study, worship, and serving together in the body of Christ (Philippians 2:2-5, Colossians 3:16-17).
- **Godly Leadership and Submission:** Embracing God's design for marital roles, where husbands lead with servant leadership and wives support and submit with respect and humility (Ephesians 5:22-24, 1 Peter 3:1-7).
- **Glorifying God:** Ultimately, the blueprint for a Christ--centered biblical marriage aims to glorify God in all aspects of the relationship, reflecting His love, grace, and truth to the world (1 Corinthians 10:31, Colossians 3:17).

By aligning with these biblical principles, you can build a strong foundation for your marriage, rooted in God's design and empowered by His presence and guidance.

3. **FORGIVENESS AND GRACE**

- Matthew 6:14-15, *"For if you forgive men when they sin against you, your heavenly Father will also forgive you. But if you do not forgive men their sins, your Father will not forgive your sins"*(NIV).
- 1 John 1:9, *"If we confess our sins, he is faithful and just and will forgive us our sins and purify us from all unrighteousness"* (NIV).
- Isaiah 43:25-26, *"I, even I, am he who blots out your transgressions, for my own sake, and remembers your sins no more. Review the past for me, let us argue the matter together; state the case for your innocence"* (NIV).
- Acts 3:19, *"Repent, then, and turn to God, so that your sins may be wiped out, that times of refreshing may come from the Lord"* (NIV).
- Isaiah 1:18, *"Come now, let us reason together," says the LORD. "Though your sins are like scarlet, they shall be as white as snow; though they are red as crimson, they shall be like wool"* (ESV).
- 2 Corinthians 5:17, *"Therefore, if anyone is in Christ, the new creation has come: The old has gone, the new is here"* (NIV)!
- Ephesians 1:7, *"In him we have redemption through his blood, the forgiveness of sins, in accordance with the riches of God's grace"* (NIV).
- Hebrews 10:17, *Then he adds: "Their sins and lawless acts I will remember no more."*
- Daniel 9:9, *"The Lord our God is merciful and forgiving, even though we have rebelled against him"* (NIV);

- Colossians 1:13-14, *"For he has rescued us from the dominion of darkness and brought us into the kingdom of the Son he loves, in whom we have redemption, the forgiveness of sins"* (NIV).
- Psalm 103:12, *"as far as the east is from the west, so far has he removed our transgressions from us"* (NIV).
- Numbers 14:19-21, *"In accordance with your great love, forgive the sin of these people, just as you have pardoned them from the time they left Egypt until now." The LORD replied, "I have forgiven them, as you asked. Nevertheless, as surely as I live and as surely as the glory of the LORD fills the whole earth"* (NIV).
- Micah 7:18-19, *"Who is a God like you, who pardons sin and forgives the transgression of the remnant of his inheritance? You do not stay angry forever but delight to show mercy. You will again have compassion on us; you will tread our sins underfoot and hurl all our iniquities into the depths of the sea"* (NIV).
- Matthew 6:9-15, *"This, then, is how you should pray: "Our Father in heaven, hallowed be your name, your kingdom come, your will be done on earth as it is in heaven. Give us today our daily bread. Forgive us our debts, as we also have forgiven our debtors. And lead us not into temptation, but deliver us from the evil one.' For if you forgive men when they sin against you, your heavenly Father will also forgive you. But if you do not forgive men their sins, your Father will not forgive your sins"* (NIV).
- Mark 11:25, *"And when you stand praying, if you hold anything against anyone, forgive him, so that your Father in heaven may forgive you your sins"* (NIV).
- Matthew 26:28, *"This is my blood of the covenant, which is poured out for many for the forgiveness of sins"* (NIV).

4. **GOD'S BLUEPRINT FOR MARRIAGE**

- Genesis 2:24, *"Therefore a man shall leave his father and his mother and hold fast to his wife, and they shall become one flesh"* (ESV).
- Malachi 2:16, *"For I hate divorce, says the Lord, the God of Israel"* (NLT).
- Ephesians 5:31-32, *"Therefore a man shall leave his father and mother and hold fast to his wife, and the two shall become one flesh. This mystery is profound, and I am saying that it refers to Christ and the church"* (ESV).
- Matthew 19:4-6, *"Have you not read that he who created them from the beginning made them male and female, and said, 'Therefore a man shall leave his father and his mother and hold fast to his wife, and the two shall become one flesh'? So they are no longer two but one flesh. What therefore God has joined together, let not man separate"* (ESV).

- 1 Corinthians 7:10-11, *"To the married I give this charge (not I, but the Lord): the wife should not separate from her husband (but if she does, she should remain unmarried or else be reconciled to her husband), and the husband should not divorce his wife"* (ESV).

5. **BIBLICAL FOUNDATION OUTLINED IN SCRIPTURE**

    - Genesis 2:24, *"Therefore a man shall leave his father and his mother and hold fast to his wife, and they shall become one flesh"* (ESV).
    - 1 Corinthians 7:2, *"But because of the temptation to sexual immorality, each man should have his own wife and each woman her own husband"* (ESV).
    - Proverbs 18:22, *"He who finds a wife finds a good thing and obtains favor from the Lord"* (ESV).

6. **COMMUNICATION IN MARRIAGE**

    - Proverbs 12:18, *"Some people make cutting remarks, but the wise words bring healing"* (NLT).
    - Proverbs 17:27, *"A truly wise person uses few words; a person with understanding is even-tempered"* (NLT).
    - Proverbs 18:13, *"Spouting off before listening to the facts is both shameful and foolish"* (NLT).
    - Psalm 19:14, *"May the words of my mouth and the meditations of my heart be pleasing to you, O Lord, my Rock, and Redeemer"* (NLT).
    - Proverbs 20:19, *"A gossip goes around telling secrets, so don't hang around with chatters"* (NLT).
    - Matthew 7:3, *"and why worry about a speck in your friend's eye when you have a log in your own"* (NLT).
    - James 1:19, *"Understand this, dear brothers and sisters: you must all be quick to listen, slow to speak, and slow to anger"* (NLT).

52 WEEKLY AFFIRMATIONS OF YOUR IDENTITY IN CHRIST A FULL YEAR OF POWERFUL DECLARATIONS

(Scripture taken from the NIV)

HOW TO USE:

Start Each Week with Intention
At the beginning of each week, read and reflect on the affirmation provided. Make it a goal to keep this reminder at the forefront of your mind throughout the week.

Speak the Declaration Daily
Begin each day by speaking the weekly affirmation aloud. Repeat it in your morning prayers, during quiet moments, or whenever you need encouragement. Speaking God's truth over your life helps reinforce your identity in Christ.

Meditate on the Scripture
Each affirmation is rooted in a specific Bible verse. Take time to read the full verse in your Bible, meditate on its meaning, and ask God to deepen your understanding of what it means for your life.

Journal Your Reflections
Use a journal to write down how the weekly declaration applies to your life. Record any insights, prayers, or experiences that highlight how this affirmation impacts your relationship with Christ.

Pray with the Affirmation
Incorporate the weekly reminder into your prayers, asking God to help you see yourself as He sees you. Pray that this truth will take root in your heart and influence your thoughts, actions, and decisions.

Share and Encourage Others
Share the weekly affirmation with a friend, spouse, or family member. Encouraging one another in Christ's truths can help deepen your faith together and provide accountability.

Reflect at Week's End
At the end of the week, reflect on how the affirmation has shaped your thoughts and actions. Write down any changes you noticed or challenges you faced in living out your identity in Christ.

Move to the Next Reminder
At the start of a new week, move on to the next affirmation. Carry forward any truths or insights from the previous week, allowing the series of reminders to build upon each other throughout the year.

By following these steps each week, you'll experience a year of growth, transformation, and a stronger understanding of who you are in Christ. Let each reminder anchor you in God's love and truth as you journey through all 52 affirmations.

WEEKLY AFFIRMATIONS:

ONE: 2 CORINTHIANS 5:17 - NEW
I am a new creation in Christ; the old has gone, and the new is here.

TWO: GALATIANS 2:20 - CRUCIFIED
I am crucified with Christ, and I no longer live, but Christ lives in me.

THREE: EPHESIANS 1:3-4 - CHOSEN
I am chosen in Christ before the creation of the world to be holy and blameless in God's sight.

FOUR: EPHESIANS 2:10 - MASTERPIECE
I am God's handiwork, created in Christ Jesus to do good works.

FIVE: 1 PETER 2:9 - ROYALTY
I am part of a chosen people, a royal priesthood, a holy nation, God's special possession.

SIX: ROMANS 8:1 - FREE
I am not condemned, for I am in Christ Jesus.

SEVEN: JOHN 1:12 - CHILD
I am a child of God, given the right to become part of His family.

EIGHT: ROMANS 8:37 - CONQUEROR
I am more than a conqueror through Christ, who loves me.

NINE: COLOSSIANS 3:3 - HIDDEN
I am hidden with Christ in God, and my life belongs to Him.

TEN: PHILIPPIANS 3:20 - CITIZEN
I am a citizen of Heaven, eagerly awaiting my Savior, the Lord Jesus Christ.

ELEVEN: COLOSSIANS 2:9-10 - COMPLETE
I am complete in Christ, who is the head of every power and authority.

TWELVE: EPHESIANS 1:7 - REDEEMED
I am redeemed through Christ's blood and forgiven of my sins according to the riches of God's grace.

THIRTEEN: ROMANS 6:6 - LIBERATED
I am liberated from sin, for my old self was crucified with Christ.

FOURTEEN: 1 CORINTHIANS 6:19-20 - TEMPLE
I am a temple of the Holy Spirit, bought with a price and belonging to God.

FIFTEEN: 1 JOHN 3:1 - BELOVED
I am loved greatly by God, and He calls me His child.

SIXTEEN: 2 TIMOTHY 1:7 - EMPOWERED
I am empowered with a spirit of power, love, and self-discipline.

SEVENTEEN: EPHESIANS 2:19 - FAMILY
I am a member of God's household, no longer a foreigner or stranger.

EIGHTEEN: COLOSSIANS 1:13-14 - RESCUED
I am rescued from the dominion of darkness and brought into the kingdom of God's beloved Son.

NINETEEN: ROMANS 8:17 - HEIR
I am an heir of God and co-heir with Christ, sharing in His glory.

TWENTY: 1 PETER 1:23 - REBORN
I am born again, not of perishable seed but of imperishable, through the living and enduring Word of God.

TWENTY-ONE: EPHESIANS 1:13-14 - SEALED
I am sealed with the promised Holy Spirit, included in Christ, and guaranteed my inheritance.

TWENTY-TWO: ROMANS 5:8 - LOVED
I am loved by God, who demonstrated His love by Christ dying for me while I was still a sinner.

TWENTY-THREE: JOHN 15:15 - FRIEND
I am called a friend of Christ, who has made known to me everything He learned from the Father.

TWENTY-FOUR: PHILIPPIANS 4:13 - STRENGTHENED
I am strengthened to do all things through Christ, Who empowers me.

TWENTY-FIVE: COLOSSIANS 3:12 - CHOSEN
I am chosen, holy, and dearly loved by God, and I am called to clothe myself with compassion, kindness, humility, gentleness, and patience.

TWENTY-SIX: ROMANS 8:15 - ADOPTED
I am a child of God, adopted by Him, and I call Him "Abba, Father."

TWENTY-SEVEN: 1 CORINTHIANS 1:30 - REDEEMED
I am in Christ Jesus, who has become for me wisdom from God—my righteousness, holiness, and redemption.

TWENTY-EIGHT: EPHESIANS 3:12 - CONFIDENT
I am able to approach God with freedom and confidence through faith in Christ.

TWENTY-NINE: 2 CORINTHIANS 5:21 - RIGHTEOUS
I am the righteousness of God in Christ Jesus.

THIRTY: 1 JOHN 4:4 - OVERCOMER
I am an overcomer, for He who is in me is greater than he who is in the world.

THIRTY-ONE: EPHESIANS 1:5 - PREDESTINED
I am predestined for adoption to sonship through Jesus Christ in accordance with God's pleasure and will.

THIRTY-TWO: 1 CORINTHIANS 15:57 - VICTORIOUS
I am victorious through my Lord Jesus Christ, who gives me victory.

THIRTY-THREE: ROMANS 8:16-17 - HEIR
I am a co-heir with Christ, sharing in His sufferings and His glory.

THIRTY-FOUR: 1 THESSALONIANS 5:5 - LIGHT
I am a child of the light and a child of the day; I do not belong to the night or to the darkness.

THIRTY-FIVE: COLOSSIANS 3:1 - RAISED
I am raised with Christ, and I set my heart on things above, where Christ is seated at the right hand of God.

THIRTY-SIX: EPHESIANS 2:6 - SEATED
I am seated with Christ in the Heavenly realms because of God's great love and grace.

THIRTY-SEVEN: COLOSSIANS 1:22 - BLAMELESS
I am holy in God's sight, without blemish, and free from accusation because of Christ's sacrifice.

THIRTY-EIGHT: 2 CORINTHIANS 1:21-22 - ANOINTED
I am established, anointed, and sealed by God, who has given me His Spirit in my heart as a deposit.

THIRTY-NINE: 1 JOHN 5:18 - PROTECTED
I am born of God, and the evil one cannot touch me.

FORTY: 1 CORINTHIANS 6:17 - UNITED
I am united with the Lord, and I am one with Him in spirit.

FORTY-ONE: 1 PETER 5:10 - RESTORED
I am being restored, strengthened, and established by the God of all grace after I have suffered a little while.

FORTY-TWO: ROMANS 15:13 - JOYFUL
I am filled with all joy and peace as I trust in God, and I overflow with hope by the power of the Holy Spirit.

FORTY - THREE: EPHESIANS 5:8 - LIGHTBEARER
I am light in the Lord; I live as a child of light.

FORTY-FOUR: MATTHEW 5:14 - LIGHT
I am the light of the world, shining with the love and truth of Christ.

FORTY-FIVE: JOHN 15:5 - FRUITFUL
I am a branch of the true vine, Jesus Christ, and I bear fruit as I remain in Him.

FORTY-SIX: 1 CORINTHIANS 3:16 - INDWELT
I am God's temple, and His Spirit dwells within me.

FORTY-SEVEN: 2 CORINTHIANS 3:18 - TRANSFORMED
I am being transformed into Christ's image with ever-increasing glory, which comes from the Lord, who is the Spirit.

FORTY-EIGHT: ROMANS 5:1 - JUSTIFIED
I am justified by faith, and I have peace with God through my Lord Jesus Christ.

FORTY-NINE: PHILIPPIANS 1:6 - CONFIDENT
I am confident that He who began a good work in me will carry it on to completion until the day of Christ Jesus.

FIFTY: 1 PETER 1:5 - SHIELDED
I am shielded by God's power through faith, ready for salvation to be revealed in the last time.

FIFTY-ONE: 2 TIMOTHY 2:1 - STRONG
I am strong in the grace that is in Christ Jesus.

FIFTY-TWO: ROMANS 8:2 - FREED
I am set free from the law of sin and death through the Spirit who gives life in Christ Jesus.

THE DASH

(A poem by Linda Ellis)

I read of a man who stood to speak
at the funeral of a friend.
He referred to the dates on the tombstone
from the beginning… to the end.

He noted that first came the date of birth
and spoke the following date with tears,
but he said what mattered most of all
was the dash between those years.

For that dash represents all the time
that they spent time alive on Earth.
And now only those who loved them
know what that little line is worth.

For it matters not, how much we own,
the cars…the house…the cash.
What matters is how we live and love
and how we spend our dash.

So, think about this long and hard.
Are there things you'd like to change?
For you never know how much time is left
that can still be rearranged.

If we could just slow down enough
to consider what's true and real
and always try to understand
the way other people feel.

And be less quick to anger
and show appreciation more
and love the people in our lives
like we've never loved before.

If we treat each other with respect
and more often wear a smile,
remembering that this special dash
might only last a little while.

So, when your eulogy is being read,
with your life's actions to rehash…
would you be proud of the things they say
about how you spent YOUR dash?[17]

Copyright © Linda Ellis

VISION PLANNING FOR YOUR MARRIAGE

Whether you're newlyweds, seasoned partners, or somewhere in between, we believe that there's always room to deepen your connection, nurture intimacy, and build a marriage that honors God and reflects His design. So, come as you are, with all your hopes, dreams, and challenges, and let's embark on this journey together, hand in hand, toward a brighter, more fulfilling future in Christ.

The purpose of vision planning for your marriage is to provide a blueprint for your journey together, guiding you toward shared goals, values, and aspirations. It helps you align your priorities, make intentional choices, and navigate through life's challenges with clarity and unity. By crafting a vision for your marriage, you create a foundation for growth, resilience, and fulfillment, fostering a deeper connection and sense of purpose in your relationship.

A. Importance of Having a Vision Plan for Your Marriage

Having a vision for yourself and your marriage is like setting a course for your journey together—a blueprint that guides your actions, choices, and priorities toward a shared destination. Just as a ship needs a clear direction to navigate through stormy seas, you need a vision to navigate the challenges and joys of married life. In this chapter, we'll explore the importance of crafting a vision for yourself and your marriage, discovering how it can bring clarity, purpose, and unity to your relationship.

B. Overview of the Process

In the vision planning process for marriage, you will embark on a purposeful journey of co-creation, exploration, and alignment toward a shared future. Through intentional dialogue, reflection, and goal-setting, spouses will articulate their individual aspirations and values, as well as their collective dreams and priorities for marriage. Guided by the principles of communication, unity, and faith, this process will empower you to create a vision that reflects your unique identity as a couple and aligns with God's design for your relationship. With a clear vision in hand, you will be equipped to navigate life's challenges, celebrate its joys, and journey together with purpose, intentionality, and unity.

To embark on the vision planning process for your marriage, you will need to set aside dedicated time and space for intentional reflection, discussion, and planning.

Here's an overview of what the process may entail:

1. *Set aside time*: Schedule dedicated sessions where you and your spouse can focus solely on vision planning. Choose a time when you're both relaxed, unhurried, and able to engage in meaningful conversation.
2. *Create a comfortable environment*: Find a quiet and comfortable space where you can have open and honest discussions without distractions. Consider lighting candles, playing soft music, or creating a cozy atmosphere to foster intimacy and connection.
3. *Start with prayer*: Begin each session with prayer, inviting God's presence and guidance into your conversation. Ask for wisdom, clarity, and unity as you embark on this journey together.
4. *Reflect individually*: Take time to reflect individually on your personal values, aspirations, and dreams for your marriage. Consider journaling, meditation, or prayer to explore your thoughts and feelings.
5. *Share and discuss*: Come together to share your reflections with each other. Listen attentively to your spouse's perspective, thoughts, and desires, and express your own with honesty and vulnerability.
6. *Identify common themes*: Look for common themes, values, and goals that emerge from your individual reflections. Celebrate areas of alignment and explore areas of difference with curiosity and openness.
7. *Craft a shared vision*: Based on your shared values and aspirations, work together to craft a shared vision statement for your marriage. This statement should encapsulate your hopes, dreams, and commitments to each other.
8. *Set goals and action steps*: Break down your vision into actionable goals and steps that you can take together to bring it to fruition. Consider short-term and long-term objectives that align with your vision and values.
9. *Regularly review and update*: Schedule regular check-ins to review your progress, reassess your goals, and make any necessary adjustments to your vision and action plan.
10. *Celebrate your progress*: Celebrate milestones, achievements, and growth along the way. Take time to acknowledge and appreciate the journey you're on together and the blessings that come from aligning your marriage with God's design.

By following these steps and committing to the vision planning process together, you and your spouse can lay a solid foundation for a marriage that is grounded in purpose, unity, and God's design.

CORE VALUES FOR YOU AND YOUR FUTURE TOGETHER

Love Authenticity Perseverance Humility Open-mindedness Empowerment Harmony Justice Kindness Optimism Self-discipline Spirituality Teamwork Wellness Independence Adventure Creativity Balance Determination Resilience Stewardship Respect Trust Communication Faith Integrity Compassion Forgiveness Family Unity Commitment Growth Honesty Empathy Gratitude Responsibility Loyalty Patience Flexibility Generosity

INSTRUCTIONS FOR IDENTIFYING CORE VALUES:

Individual Reflection:

1. Take some time to reflect on your personal values and what matters most to you in life.
2. Research the definitions to confirm that these values are truly significant to you.
3. Consider experiences, beliefs, and principles that have shaped your values over time.
4. Make a list of values that resonate with you, ranking them in order of importance.

Couple Reflection:

Combine your individual responses into a unified list tailored specifically for your marriage. Identify shared values and craft a mission statement that resonates with both of you. Place it in a prominent location as a constant reminder of your shared vision for moving forward together.

Our mission statement:

ENDNOTES

1. Father-Daughter Connection, MariLouise Rust 1998 NCCA pg. 32
2. Forgiveness Prayer adapted from Matthew 6:9-14 NIV and Wellspring Ministries; Anchorage, Alaska: https://akwellspring.com/
3. Forgiveness Prayer adapted from Matthew 6:9-14 NIV and Wellspring Ministries; Anchorage, Alaska: https://akwellspring.com/
4. https://www.michelangelo.org/the-creation-of-adam.jsp
5. Overture, "I Am (Creation)" Music Inspired by the Story Album, Bernie Herms, Sparrow Joint Venture, 2011, open.spotify.com/track/5R3Ob4dcnqx5fypl4ZIsfN?si=ffff192734fd4106
6. Assisi, S. F. O. (2023). *The Writings of Saint Francis of Assisi: Timeless Teachings of Compassion and Humility from a Revered Saint.* Good Press.
7. Niebuhr, R. (1986). *The Essential Reinhold Niebuhr: Selected Essays and Addresses.* Yale University Press.
8. https://5lovelanguages.com/quizzes/love-language
9. *A quote by Jim Rohn.* (n.d.). https://www.goodreads.com/quotes/1798-you-are-the-average-of-the-five-people-you-spend
10. Npr. (2015, September 8). "Don Quixote" Speaks To The "Quality Of Being A Dreamer." NPR. https://www.npr.org/2015/09/08/438633625/don-quixote-speaks-to-the-quality-of-being-a-dreamer#:~:text=One%20must%20live%20life%20in,according%20to%20Professor%20Ilan%20Stavans.
11. https://firmisrael.org/learn/the-meaning-of-shalom/
12. https://thinkaboutsuchthings.com/christian-morning-routine/
13. Ellis, L. M., & Anderson, M. (2005). *The Dash: Making a Difference with Your Life.*
14. Forgiveness Prayer adapted from Matthew 6:9-14 NIV and Wellspring Ministries; Anchorage, Alaska: https://akwellspring.com/

15. Assisi, S. F. O. (2023). *The Writings of Saint Francis of Assisi: Timeless Teachings of Compassion and Humility from a Revered Saint.* Good Press.
16. Niebuhr, R. (1986). *The Essential Reinhold Niebuhr: Selected Essays and Addresses.* Yale University Press.
17. Ellis, L. M., & Anderson, M. (2005). *The Dash: Making a Difference with Your Life.*

ABOUT THE AUTHOR

Dr. Deborah Skomba, the founder of Heart-to-Heart Ministry and Coaching, specializes in Christ–centered marriage counseling, using biblical truths and strength-based techniques to nurture healing and authenticity in relationships. With over 40 years of personal marital experience, she empowers women to become catalysts for positive change in their marriages through her five H.E.A.R.T. power tools—Healing, Empowerment, Authenticity, Restoration, and Trust.

She serves couples and individual women by helping them navigate positive change in their marriages and relationships through biblical truths and strength-based approaches.

Check out Deborah's other published books, *A Better Marriage Prayer Journal: 31 Days of Scriptural Reflections and Guided Questions for Deepening Your Connection*, and *The Road to Bethlehem: An Advent Journey*.

Visit www.h2hcoaching.com for more information.

OTHER TITLES
BY DR. DEBORAH SKOMBA

A Better Marriage Prayer Journal

31 days of Scriptural Reflections and Guided Questions for Deepening Your Connection.

The Road to Bethlehem

An Advent Journey

www.ingramcontent.com/pod-product-compliance
Lightning Source LLC
Chambersburg PA
CBHW082231180426
43200CB00037B/2771